Praise for *Awakening to*

Kerri's raw courage and vulnerable transparency blaze a trail for any woman on a healing journey. *Awakening to Me* is a magnificent book that takes us behind the scenes of transformation, and shows how even the most difficult situations can be the fodder for finding oneself. Let Kerri's book guide you to find your independence and self-love.

— HeatherAsh Amara, author of *The Toltec Path of Transformation* and *Warrior Goddess Training*

In *Awakening To Me*, Kerri shares her intimate and difficult personal and spiritual journey to identify and express her authentic being into the world. Her story is engaging, sometimes disturbing, yet with a clear underlying thread of compassion for herself and others also engaged in their own struggle with borderline personality disorder. In her words, she seeks to give voice to those who have no voice.

Her life voyage takes her through light and darkness, to amazing heights and agonizing lows. In her world travels she meets with some of the teachers who have helped shape the views of spiritual development for a generation. Each has something to share with her that may shed light upon your own path, as well.

It has been my pleasure and honor to walk with Kerri through some of her journey. I heartily recommend this book to you as a tool for your own amazing self-exploration. Among these pages you will find a courageous and dedicated explorer of life and spirit.

— Gerry Starnes, M.Ed, author of *Spirit Paths: The Quest for Authenticity*

Awakening to Me

One Woman's Journey to Self Love

Kerri Hummingbird Lawnsby

First published in the United States of America by Siwarkinte Publishing

Awakening to Me: One Woman's Journey to Self-Love
Kerri Hummingbird Lawnsby

Cover design by © Kerri Lawnsby (aka Kerri Hummingbird Lawnsby)
Illustration by © Kerri Lawnsby (aka Kerri Hummingbird Lawnsby)
Photograph of Kerri Hummingbird Lawnsby by Lara Falardeau.
www.clickedbylara.com

This book may be ordered directly from Amazon.com.

ISBN-13: 978-0615897981
ISBN-10: 0615897983

For more information about Kerri Hummingbird Lawnsby, visit:
Web: www.kerrilawnsby.com
Twitter: @KerriHummingbrd
Facebook: Kerri.Hummingbird
Pinterest: kerrihummingbrd
YouTube: Kerri Hummingbird

I dedicate this book to you, to your beautiful soul waiting to awaken from the darkness. Open your heart and your mind dear one... then open your eyes and see your reflection. You are divine.

♥

"You can search throughout the entire universe for someone who is more deserving of your love and affection than you are yourself, and that person is not to be found anywhere.

You yourself, as much as anybody in the entire universe deserve your love and affection."
— *Buddha*

"There are only two mistakes one can make along the road to truth; not going all the way, and not starting."
—*Buddha*

Acknowledgements

From the bottom of my heart, I thank Spirit for guiding me each and every day on the journey of my life. I thank my sons, Garrett and Tanner, for endless support and thousands of I love you's. I thank my parents for supporting my growth into a woman and mother, even if they do not completely understand all the things I seek and do. I thank my soul daughter, Shana, for being the daughter I dreamed I would have. I thank my friends for understanding my struggle yet holding me accountable for my healing. I thank my mentors—Gerry Starnes, Cecilia Zuniga, Chrispy Bhagat Singh, HeatherAsh Amara, and the amazing faculty at the Four Winds Society—for opening doors to healing that have transformed my life entirely. I thank the many people who entered my life during this transformational period, most of whom read and consented to the publishing of this story. Gratitude to my best friends Marques Harper and Dorothy Sloan for providing invaluable editorial feedback, as well as Gerry Starnes, Chrispy Bhagat Singh, and HeatherAsh Amara for mentoring me through my healing journey and going the extra mile to review my manuscript.

Thank you to Alberto Villoldo for following his heart and intuition to learn from the indigenous shamans in South America, and to persevere to develop an amazing body of shamanic healing practices that have forever changed the course of my life. Endless gratitude and overflowing munay. Because of your courage and conviction, I am no longer lost in the dark: I am a lighthouse of hope that people can find the way home to their essential selves.

Most of all, I thank myself for slogging through swampy murky waters fearlessly and believing there would be joy and love at the other side.

❤

Why

This journey begins with a single step: a decision to share openly my personal experience in the hopes that you might benefit from hearing it. That you might realize: *You are not alone.*

Along my journey, Spirit guided me to the realization that I have a gift: *courage.*

"The root of the word courage is cor—the Latin word for heart. In one of its earliest forms, the word courage had a very different definition than it does today. Courage originally meant 'To speak one's mind by telling all one's heart.'" — *Brené Brown*[1]

By sharing my story, I give you permission to share yours. I open the door in a darkened room, and let the summer sunshine dispel the shadows so that you may see that there is no shame in your experience—there is only the opportunity to learn and grow into the person you were meant to be.

Each one of us on this planet is meant to be here; otherwise, we would not have been given this precious gift of *Life*.

There have been times in my existence that I did not feel the preciousness of Life; rather, I felt its burdens and heaviness and pain.

I am here to tell you, there is hope. There is a path to a joyful existence. And it can happen for you even if you currently exist in darkness.

I have felt absolute terror about sharing my story with you. I have felt fear about what you will think of me. I have felt fear about what you will say about me to my children, to my parents, to my face, or worse, behind my back. This is my fear. My fear wants to keep me in the darkness living in shame. I am writing this story because **I refuse to let fear win.** This book is my authentic story. It is me. And to love myself, I have to let my story live in the light, I have to accept myself for the path I have had to walk.

This story is important to be heard. As I have shared my story privately throughout the years, I have heard from so many other souls that have struggled with sexual abuse as a child or adult, at the hands of family members and trusted loved ones: brothers, sisters, fathers, mothers, cousins, step-parents, and the list goes on. This is *love abuse*. It needs to stop.

I do not hold a master's degree or doctorate. I am not trained in psychotherapy (although, I think with the 30 some-odd years I have spent on a couch, I should have earned an honorary degree by now).

I am not healed, I am not cured: I simply have awareness of my patterns of thinking and behavior, and I have the capacity to make different choices.

I am merely a student of life, a master and student of my own experience. And because I have struggled, I have compassion for your struggle. But you might say, "You don't even know me. How can you care?"

I care because you are part of my Universe. We are made of the same material—you and I. We are from the same Source. If I can touch your heart, and help you heal even a little of your pain, one battle in the war against fear and shame has been won, and we have given love the advantage for a moment in time. All love needs is a crack—that's how the light gets in. 2

I know you can find your own joy. I know you can learn to love yourself.

❤

As I sit on my front porch I see him. His long slender scaly body stretched cool against the warm concrete of the step, his viridian neck extended high, his head alert but relaxed in the sunlight.

An unexpected visitor: the Snake.

A Soul In Crisis

ର the journey begins in shadows ର

I am misery. I am surrounded by darkness. I am abandoned in my treachery. I am inconsolable. I cry hot tears from the bottom of my soul, and they scorch my eyes. My thoughts are whips and knives that slash my self-worth until there is nothing left but a bloody aching mass. I want to die. I cannot see light. Nor hope. Nor peace of any kind. I am trapped inside a hell of my own making. And I cannot escape.

My cousin's voice is like the seductive drip of heroin into my veins. His strong and gentle hands cradle my head as his tongue caresses mine, then his fingers trace the contour of my neck down to my shoulders where he brushes aside the bows that hold up my halter top and it slides down as his tongue follows, wrapping around my nipple as desire swells from the deepest part of me. I am suspended in thick sweet honey.

The memory of our intimacy has become an endless loop of sensations for my starving heart, a loop that is always completed by the grand finale: a darkening and crushing wisdom that our love cannot be. That our love is wrong.

Still I yearn for him. This unexpected romance somehow blossomed in the back alley of my marriage, and after nearly two decades of making it work I see that the foundation of the life my husband and I built together has irreparable damage. My cousin, who I have known since we were children but only reconnected with in the past year, points it out to me, defending my honor: "I don't like the way he treats you. You deserve so much more Kerri." Somehow this kindness from a trusted soul opens the door, and we cross the line into a forbidden world.

ର

The day is finally here…
the day planned for over a month in secret conversations over text
messages and phone calls…
The day long awaited and anticipated…
The day we would make love for the first time.
I knock on the door and as he opens it our eyes lock together in steamy
desire.
I melt into his arms. His lips are soft as they meet mine, his tongue
explores my mouth with passionate yearning and deft expression.
He knows what he is doing to me.
I have known him all my life and trust him completely.
I dissolve into bliss.

ભ

Now he has ended it after a mere 2 months, my thirst for love and romance unquenched. I become desperate for my cousin's attention. I promise things I have no business promising.

"We can go back to the way we were."

I send him kind thoughts over text message in hopes of a response. "Missing you today. Wishing you the best." When I do not hear from him, I obsess. I keep watching my cellphone to see if the light blinks, to see if he has messaged me. A day goes by and I am crazed. Why doesn't he respond? Does he care for me at all?

I am abandoned.

Eventually he calls. He says he cares for me but he cannot help me to get over him. He says this affair, and continued contact with him, is not good for me, and what we have done is morally wrong. It is unnatural for cousins to have an affair as we have, he says. He has put his feelings for me in a box and left it for God.

He has thrown me out. Like trash.

I am devastated. I am filled with shame. I am savage at the loss of his love. In my mind's eye, I streak blood across my face and storm screaming with axe in hand to exact revenge. In reality, I sit crying at my desk while futilely trying to work on consulting projects for clients. I am hopeless.

I hear a Nine Inch Nails' song, and repeat it over and over and over in my mind. The song is so profound and exactly how I feel. I text him the lyrics.

> *Well the tiniest little dot caught my eye*
> *and it turned out to be a scab*
>
> *And I had this funny feeling like I just knew*
> *it's something bad*
>
> *I just couldn't leave it alone,*
> *I kept picking at the scab*
>
> *It was a doorway trying to seal itself shut*
> *But I climbed through*
>
> *Now I am somewhere I am not supposed to be,*
> *and I can see things I know I really shouldn't see*
>
> *And now I know why, now, now, now I know why Things aren't as pretty*
> *On the inside*[3]

I want to die. I am afraid I might actually try to kill myself. In a moment of weakness, in fear for my life, I tell my husband what has happened. He calls me right after I have talked with my cousin and my heart is breaking and my husband can hear it in my voice. I confess. My husband listens, absorbs the wound, and turns the other cheek. He tells me he is not worried about this affair, because it has been with my cousin. It is a forbidden love that will never come to light.

That night, my husband acts like it's no big deal what has happened with me and my cousin. In fact, if it makes me happy, I can keep doing it. It's not like I'll leave my husband for my cousin.

୦୫

My shadow is long, deep, and wide. I can't stop thinking of my cousin which makes me angry at myself, and desperate. But I can't stop thinking about the love between us. Why is our love wrong? It feels right. It feels more right than anything I've ever felt in my life. I text him, trying to convince him…

> *Meet me in outer space*
> *We could spend the night*
> *Watch the earth come up*
>
> *I've grown tired of that place*
> *Won't you come with me?*
> *We could start again*[4]

He is tempted and almost bites, texting me how much he misses being with me. But then he rejects me all over again. He tells me our love is evil; he fills me with agonizing *shame*. I cry all day at home while my children are at school. I hear songs that make my heart break. I feel connection as Kanye West croons Heartless…

> *In the night I hear 'em talk, the coldest story ever told*
> *Somewhere far along this road he lost his soul*
> *To a woman so heartless*
> *How could you be so heartless?*[5]

“”

I love him, and I hate him. Over the months that pass, I try to return to being family, but I can't stop wanting his love and intimacy. I feel addicted to him.

Around this time, I have dinner with some artist friends, and one of them tells a story about an acquaintance in the army who keeps re-enlisting for service. We keep wondering what would make a person continue to sign up to go into hostile situations where it was necessary to kill and kill again, and again?

I have an epiphany. If this soldier stops killing, if he returns to a civilized life, he will have to face his demons, he will have to face himself in the mirror and settle up with God.

If this affair ends, I will have to face the truth of my treachery: *I betrayed myself. I betrayed my family.*

Suggestions

If you are in crisis right now, consider trying these home remedies to regain sanity and composure. Just know: <u>this too shall pass</u>. ♥

Get Outside! *Fresh air is incredibly useful for shifting mood. I know you want to stay in a dark room and sulk, but get outside in the sunshine. Now! Breathe the sunshine in <u>deeply</u>. Stop holding onto your pain. Let it go.*

Move the Energy! *Walk, run, bike, or do yoga. Do some sort of exercise daily. Even if you do not feel like it, force yourself to do it. Depression feeds off stagnation. When you move the energy, you will elevate your mood and make space for peace. At the lowest point in my journey, I would run for at least 6 miles, my mind churning over my pain, until finally I felt peace and could see the sunshine.*

Listen to Soothing Music! *One choice I made that prolonged my grief was listening to music that resonated with my own sorrow and desperation. Turn off the radio or carefully choose music to soothe your aching soul. I recommend instrumental music without lyrics.*

Breathe! *Breathe in deeply while thinking "Peace" entering your body, breathe out in a forceful burst while visualizing "Pain" being tossed out of your body like phlegm. Breathing practices, such as those done with yoga, activate communication pathways between the mind and the body that have positive impact on your brain by calming your stress. If this is a new concept for you, suspend disbelief and try it!*

Cry! No matter the cause of your angst, let yourself grieve. Allow yourself to feel the pain. Go deep into the bowels of your home, into a dark closet where no one will hear you, and <u>SCREAM and CRY</u>. This part is very frightening because the emotion can be so absolutely consuming and overwhelming. Allowing this expression moves the anger, sadness, and other toxic emotions out of your body. If you suppress these toxic emotions, they can end up manifesting physically in your body.

After I eventually left my husband, my doctor discovered a Texas grapefruit-sized cyst on my ovary. I nicknamed it my marriage cyst and had it removed. Do not <u>stuff</u> your emotions! Risk people thinking you're crazy for screaming in your house. You'll only hurt yourself if you don't get it out.

Quotes

"Owning our story can be hard but not nearly as difficult as spending our lives running from it. Embracing our vulnerabilities is risky but not nearly as dangerous as giving up on love and belonging and joy—the experiences that make us the most vulnerable. Only when we are brave enough to explore the darkness will we discover the infinite power of our light." — Brenè Brown[6]

"...incessant mental noise prevents you from finding that realm of inner stillness that is inseparable from Being. It also creates a false mind-made self that casts a shadow of fear and suffering." — Eckhart Tolle[7]

"You have the strength. You just don't know it yet."
— Kimberly Wharton

"A journey of a thousand miles begins with a single step."
— Laozi, Tao Te Ching[8]

"Avoid continually replaying the event, the insult, the pain over and over again, wondering how it could possibly happen to you. The disaster happened, you survived, and now it's time to get on with rebuilding." — Gerry Starnes, M.Ed[9]

"When physical or emotional pain arises, our reflex is to resist it not only by stiffening our body and contracting our muscles, but also by contracting our mind. We lose ourselves in thoughts about what is wrong, how long it will last, what we should do about it and how the pain reflects our unworthiness...Feeling fear or anger or jealousy means something is wrong with us, that we are weak or bad." — Tara Brach, Ph.D.[10]

"When you calm your disaster mind, mental chaos dissolves into a clarifying spring breeze that blows away the dust and cobwebs so that you can clearly see what your next step is." — HeatherAsh Amara[11]

"Studies are revealing that by changing the patterns of breathing it is possible to restore balance to stress response systems, calm an agitated mind, relieve symptoms of anxiety and post-traumatic stress disorder(PTSD)..." — Richard Brown and Patricia Gerbarg[12]

"Behind this so called love is all that fear of I'm not good enough, I'm not worthy. If I do get this commodity of love from the outside, I've got to hold onto it at any cost. And I'll sacrifice my truth, myself, my soul to hold onto it. Behind that is always the fear that we're gonna lose it. It's no wonder they call it hell." — Allan Hardman[13]

"Two choices - we're making one or the other in every moment... Expand into love, into the challenge, into the opportunity, into the grace ...or contract into fear, into isolation, into limitedness." — Chrispy Bhagat Singh[14]

Salvaging

After months of trying to get over the affair with my cousin, and failing, I start seeing a therapist. I am in so much pain over my love affair, over losing my lifelong relationship with my cousin, over comprehending what has happened and how we crossed that line—and I don't know what to do with these feelings. I feel shame about my actions, and tremendous loss for not having the intimacy and love I experienced from being with my cousin.

Months go by, and every visit to my therapist is simply recounting old territory in new ways; new words exchanged that touch old wounds, reinvigorating the feelings of loss and sorrow. I want to be stronger than I am. I am wandering around in the darkness in a world of pain.

If only I had never crossed the line.

ୡ

We have been trying to re-establish a family relationship, but my feelings for him have led to additional intimate transgressions the few times we have seen each other and so he puts a barrier in between us. She lives with him now. She is his woman. He casually mentions it to me over the phone. I die a thousand deaths.

I am driving back home from a business trip, sobbing, tears welling up into lakes and then spilling out over my cheeks.

My vision is so blurred I cannot see, and yet I am texting him as I drive on a remote highway between Tennessee and Texas, weaving wildly across lanes. I don't care if I crash and die. Despite my recklessness, I live. *How am I still here?*

ୡ

I cope. I stay busy. So busy I hardly spend time with my husband or sons. When I am with my family, I am gone somewhere deep inside my mind and staring at them through soulless eyes. I answer my children with uninspired *"Ohs"* and *"Uh-huhs"*... I don't know what they just said. Sometimes I come back to awareness to discover they have been telling me a story for a while; I don't know how long I have been gone. I am missing my children grow up, and I can't do anything about it. *Lights are on. No one is home.*

I am relieved to travel away for business. I want to be gone. And then when I am gone, I am lonely and sad. I wake up crying…missing *him*…missing love. One morning on the road from a hotel room in west Texas, I wake to tears and beg God for mercy and in that instant, the pain lifts and a calming peace clears the air. My tears stop.

I tape messages on my computer to remind myself to forget him.

> *Focus on the friends and family*
> *who love you most, and you will see*
> *how truly blessed you truly are.*

I talk to myself in the mirror at night, comforting myself as best I can that this too shall pass. I watch as my tired eyes cry more tears. I grow older by the minute.

I rally to put on appearances to the world. I seem happy to everyone but my closest friends. I am a wonderful actress. I play the part of the loving wife; I act interested in sex with my husband. I make a game of it with new outfits and special winks. I keep telling myself I am trying to love my husband again. That it is like those mantras: If you just keep saying them, someday you will believe the words. I tell myself it is the least I owe him. I am not worthy of anything better. For what I have done. Because he took me back.

I buy my husband new clothes and cologne. He is thrilled to get some attention from me. He is happy to have my love. I have another secret. I am dressing my husband like *him*.

At least I have stopped crying every day. I note this major milestone. It is significant to me.

છ

Things have shifted. It is as if the better I feel, the more critical and demanding my husband becomes. He is putting me in my place, keeping me aware of my mistake and my duty to him. I am frustrated to be trapped in the adulteress role. I do not want to be defined this way forever. I am starting to see a return of old behaviors from my husband. Nothing I do is right. Apparently, I turn up the heat too high on the eggs and ruin them. How can you ruin eggs? I want to escape my husband's tight critical grip.

I join a running group and start training for the Austin Marathon. I hardly notice the miles and my feet pounding the pavement; my mind is lost in yesterday, reliving the moments of my joy. I spend countless hours every week simply running around the neighborhood and park and reliving the fantasy projection of my past love experience. I escape easily into running because my husband appreciates the results to my body. I become a trophy for him: a sexy kitten that he owns.

I plunge into work and earn money to buy myself new breasts because I cringe when remembering how appalled I was when I revealed my naked breasts to my cousin. Breastfeeding my children had depleted my breasts and turned them into saggy flesh sacks. My husband is excited about the new implants that will substantially increase the size of my breasts. I will make a much better trophy now.

It is strange to be on a pedestal when I am so flawed.

ଔ

I take the risk of rejection and tell my story to my artist friend, Collin, while we are at an art show in Fort Worth. Her absolute acceptance of my journey begins a healing deep inside of me. When she says, "I understand how you feel," the shame I feel about my actions dissipates slightly, the judgments I have placed upon myself loosen their grip, and I see that I cannot possibly be the only person who has ever experienced adultery. I am starting to awaken to the reality that there are many other people who have had intimacy outside of their marriages, some even with relatives, whether consensual or otherwise.

I realize, ironically, that the very existence of soap operas is proof; my girlfriend and I laugh heartily about this, and it feels good.

I just never thought that would be me.

I thought I was a better person than that. I thought I had more integrity than to cheat on my husband. It seems otherworldly that I would choose to cheat on him with my cousin of all people. I do not understand what has happened. I am not the person I thought I was, but I accept that *I am human.*

∞

I don't know how long it has been since the affair because I have been lost somewhere other than my body. It has seemed like an eternity that I have struggled in my mind to let go of the affair, to return to a normal relationship with my cousin. There are moments I feel it is possible and we talk on the phone and everything seems fine. And then we visit with each other and *her* and the wound weeps afresh.

There is no healing these wounds.

Suggestions

Tell Your Story! You may not feel comfortable sharing your story, but this is the only way out of shame. As Brenè Brown tells us [15], shame is what keeps us from believing in ourselves, from believing we can have a different reality than we are currently experiencing. When we reach out to another person with our shame story, we invite compassion. The word compassion, at its Latin roots, means "to suffer with." When I "suffer with" another human, I realize: I am not alone in my pain. I am not the only person who suffers from human frailty.

Be in this Moment! The past is gone. No matter how much you might have enjoyed a certain feeling or experience from your past, you can never recapture that exact moment again. Trying to recapture that moment by fantasizing about it only keeps you stuck in a cycle of torment. (Trust me, I relieved my moment of passion hundreds of times a day for months, and still I could not bring it back.) Let that moment go, and begin to trust that new moments will arise that bring as much, or even more, pleasure.

Journal! If you can safely store a journal out of reach of those who should not read it, now is the time to begin journaling. Writing down the thoughts that swirl around in your head is a really useful way of becoming AWARE of them. Exposing these toxic thoughts to the light of day empowers you to dispel the fear and anxiety they generate, and offers you the opportunity to TRANSFORM these thoughts. I will write more about journaling later, but for now, simply put pen to paper and set your aching soul free on the page.

Positive Advice! Give yourself the gift of _hope_. Rather than affirmations (which can sometimes have an adverse effect), speak to yourself as you would to your best friend. If your friend was hurting, what would you tell her?

Here is the advice I wrote to myself:
"Your place is in the moment...right now.
Focus on the people who love you and want you to be a part of their lives too. When you do this, you will feel how blessed you truly are."

Quotes

"When we're looking for compassion, we need someone who embraces us for our strengths and struggles. We need to honor our struggle by sharing it with someone who has earned the right to hear it. When we're looking for compassion, it's about connecting with the right person at the right time about the right issue." — Brenè Brown [16]

"Shame works like the zoom lens on a camera. When we are feeling shame, the camera is zoomed in tight and all we see is our flawed selves, alone and struggling."
— Brené Brown [17]

"When you say to yourself the affirmation 'I am strong,' you are doing so because you have a belief that you are really weak. As a result, each time you repeat the affirmation, in a way you may be reinforcing the negative belief, and ultimately repeating the self curse."
— Gerry Starnes, M.Ed [18]

"When you dwell on the past, you sleepwalk through the present, missing connections and opportunities to make the present and future brighter."
—Kerri Hummingbird Lawnsby

"Compassion is like a mirror into which we can always look. It is like a stream that steadily carries us. It is like a cleansing fire that continually transforms us."
—Sharon Salzberg[19]

"Courage is not the towering oak that sees storms come and go; it is the fragile blossom that opens in the snow."
—Alice Mackenzie Swaim

"As the disaster scenarios of my mind unfolded one after another, and the voices of fear proved impossible to ignore, I was shocked. A bigger shock occurred when I realized that the disaster voices had always been there, chattering away. My silence had not created them but had allowed me to quiet down enough so I that I could hear what was previously below my consciousness. This was the key to learning how to shift my mind from disaster to clarity." —HeatherAsh Amara[20]

"[Vulnerability] is what actually saves the life and the soul of the individual." —Dr. Robin Smith, Super Soul Sunday, Oprah

Unfulfilled

There is a yawning black hole inside me, and I am seeking, seeking, seeking to fill it. It is so empty it aches; from the center of my being, it contracts like some massive menstrual cramp around my heart.

He is gone.

If I am still, if my mind is quiet, I feel this loss deeply and it is frightening. I am afraid my longing might swallow me whole and end my existence. I am afraid I will be forever lost in the inky shadowy blackness of my emptiness and my shame.

When I escape my fantasies, I can no longer see my cousin's face, nor remember exactly how it felt when he kissed me. My fantasy is a diluted distant version of its former Technicolor rendition, a foggy window into the past. He is slipping away into a void.

Love is gone.

Now there is only…*me.*

ॐ

Bag lady you gone hurt your back
Dragging all them bags like that
I guess nobody ever told you
All you must hold on to
Is you, is you, is you…

One day all them bags gone get in your way…
So pack light…

Bag lady you gone miss your bus
You can't hurry up
Cause you got too much stuff
When they see you comin'
Niggas take off runnin'
From you… it's true… oh yes they do

One day he gone say "you crowdin' my space"...
So pack light...

Girl I know sometimes it's hard
And we can't let go

Oh when someone hurts you oh so bad inside
You can't deny it, you can't stop crying
So ... If you start breathin'
Then you won't believe it
You'll feel so much better
(So much better baby)

Bag lady
Let it go, let it go, let it go, let it go
Girl you don't need it
I betcha love can make it better

ଔ

"Bag Lady" by Erykah Badu

I am thin. I am beautiful and shapely from running so many miles, and I am still wrong all the time in the world according to my husband. I am tired of the reminders of my failure. I am tired of trying to love someone who has endless criticism of me. I am tired of giving, giving, giving to a man who is never satisfied, never happy or at peace. I am tired of pretending to enjoy sex with him. I am desperate to feel <u>something</u>.

To feel love.

I can't stop scratching the back of my neck; there is this spot that itches incessantly just under the hairline. I scratch it so much it develops scabs which I scratch off again. Skin flakes on my shoulders, and my husband is constantly brushing them off and scolding me for scratching. Even special medicine applied to the area only works for a while. It is some kind of nervous tic.

ଔ

My husband and I have plans to go to Las Vegas for a trade show to promote my art business. I leave Texas and arrive a day before the show so I can set up my booth, and I am in Vegas for the day without my husband. After setting up my booth, I decide to head to the pool at the hotel, the Hilton on the Strip. I throw on my bikini and head to the pool where I discover a party is going on with a happy hour special: two drinks for the price of one. What fun! A release! Just what I need!

I befriend a woman at the party and she and I drink and talk. Out of nowhere, she points out this man at the bar. He's beautiful and has chocolate-colored skin and a lovely smile. She wants to kiss him, she says. So I say, "Let's go ask him! Why not?"

We walk over to this lovely dark man and tell him we think he's sexy.

I tell this man my friend would like to kiss him and would he like to kiss her as well? His face lights up with a stunning smile and he says yes. When my friend kisses him, I feel competitive and I want to kiss him.

I want the attention.

I say, "I can do a better job than that." And I do. I feel intense attraction, and so does he. There is a massive chemical interaction between us. Seeing the chemistry between us, my new friend leaves us and the lovely chocolate man says he wants to go to the hotel room. "My husband is coming soon," I say. "He'll walk in on us." And he says, "You're not the only one with a room silly."

I have drunken sex with this chocolate man; wanton, drunken sex. And it is over before it began but it is a clue of what could be with more time and less alcohol. We make plans for Monday night.

I meet my husband in our hotel room less than an hour later and have more drunken sex. He is happy to have the attention. I have guilty pleasure with my secret.

All weekend the obsession builds with my new man. I text him and when I hear his response beep back at me, I am giddy with excitement.

I even text him during dinner with my husband. And my husband notices. But I don't care. I am beyond caring. Because all that matters is the love feeling I am building inside myself, and the anticipation of more love-making.

My husband leaves for home Monday morning, and after wrapping up my trade show, I spend the night with Richard. We make love all night long. It feels absolutely wonderful. I've never had sex this fulfilling. To feel this way making love to a man—a man who clearly knows what he is doing—this is something new for me.

I am in love with this man, and making love to him. The intensity of the feeling fills me up and I float to Heaven on its waves. I forget about my cousin. He no longer matters in this moment because I have Richard.

I sleep in his arms and have the strangest dream that we are in this house together with many other people, and all of the sudden I can't find him. Where is Richard? I search everywhere for him, absolutely dismayed he has disappeared, terrified for his life. And then I find him again, and cling to him. I'm so happy. I wake up in his arms.

I'm not surprised entirely that Richard is showing me new ways to achieve pleasure with my body. I do not have a lot of experience.

∽

I met my husband when I was 22. I did not experiment with dating or having sex with different men as an adult. My sexual experience has been limited to my high school boyfriend, my college boyfriend, and my husband, with a few flings here and there.

When I dated Darren, one of a handful of black boys at my high school, the response was not welcoming in the blue-collar New England community where we lived in the late 1980s. In those days, you simply did not date outside of your race. I was told that dating a black boy made me a *nigger slut*. My classmates in upper-level honors classes never said this out loud to me the way the rougher kids at school would, but I was pretty sure the sentiments were widely shared. Darren and I had a love/hate relationship; we broke up and made up all throughout freshman and sophomore years. I was attracted to Darren because I liked the way he stood up to adversity and didn't let people push him around; I had hopes that he could turn his skills as football quarterback into a potentially incredible future. But maintaining his fierce reputation meant that Darren often turned to aggression to save face in a hostile community; and being openly infatuated with me made him feel weak. So much of our real connection happened in private, away from the eyes of white boys at school that Darren felt he had to impress. I didn't understand this at the time; his behavior just made me feel rejected and I would lash out publicly at him which would only make things worse.

Shortly before my 16th birthday, I lost my virginity to Darren because I was absolutely in love with him. I focused on all the times he was loving to me in private, all the kisses in the back stairwell at school, all the tenderness he would express to me when he told me he loved me.

After Darren got into trouble during a robbery instigated by his Caucasian white-collar friend Kevin, and ended up in juvenile detention, I was a pariah to other boys at the school. White boys simply didn't know what to do with a girl who had dated a black boy. I was angry at Darren for choosing a criminal path when he could have put his energy into being the football quarterback. He called me from juvenile detention and I broke up with him over the phone.

I lashed out by sleeping with several of his closest friends. If I was a "nigger slut" before, I really was one now. I loved Darren. He was the love of my life, so none of this behavior served to heal the pain at his loss; it only served to propel me deeper into self-loathing. I was so desperate for attention that I allowed myself to be treated poorly by boys. One boy was not circumcised and did not have good hygiene, and I gave him head even though what I saw and smelled made me want to gag. Another boy sat on my chest and pinned my arms with his legs while he thrust his penis into my mouth; I felt extremely claustrophobic and terrified by this, wrangling to break free of his hold.

My self-loathing culminated in a feeble attempt to take my life. The suicide attempt came after my Dad caught me with a boyfriend when he came home from work early. Banished to my room, I consumed a bottle of Tylenol with Codeine. When I started feeling the effects of the drugs, I got scared and told my Dad. My parents rushed me to the hospital and had my stomach pumped. I spent junior year of high school in weekly sessions with a psychiatrist who diagnosed me as manic depressive because of my wild mood swings and erratic behavior.

My parents did not know what to do with me. I alternated between being a perfect student with impeccable behavior to acting outlandishly and wildly. I met one boyfriend at a stoplight a mile from my house as he was cruising around on his motorcycle, and I disappeared with him for two days, sleeping in the basement of his uncle's house since he was also a runaway. I finally called my parents to let them know I was ok.

Senior year of high school I settled down and dated Eric, a Caucasian boy from a neighboring town who achieved the rank of Eagle Scout, because he was safe and stable. He didn't care for racism. He was my best friend, my staunchest supporter, and he helped me get my life back on track. We dated until the year after I graduated college. During this time, I stayed on the straight-laced side of life. I avoided attracting male attention by wearing baggy clothes and dresses that looked like they were from "Little House on the Prairie." Eric ended up dating a prude; I routinely denied him sex because I simply was completely uncomfortable with my sexuality. After senior year of college, we had become siblings instead of lovers; our friendship consumed the romantic relationship. We were high school sweethearts who had outgrown each other but persevered out of fear of letting go; it was time to move on.

I moved to California after our break-up, ending a year spent living with my parents. I sought a new job in a new city to start a new life. I bit off more than I could chew. If I had moved with girlfriends across the country, perhaps I would have spent my twenties exploring my sexuality and dating and learning to be independent.

I went from a stable, safe place in my life to uncharted waters and I ended up swimming with the sharks. A week after moving in to my shared flat in San Francisco, I began having sex with my roommate, Peter, who was also having sex with our other female roommate. It was my first love triangle, and it was a nightmare. I moved out and started dating Tom, my future husband, and never looked back.

Tom was not the sort of man who had meaningless sex, so he did not have a wealth of experience. He was not a shark; he was a playful silky seal. We were novices together. We dated for six months before moving in together and then bought our first home a year later. A dozen years went by and we were happy with our sexual relationship; I was content with sex being quick and heated. Although Tom encouraged experimentation, I was uncomfortable with the idea of sex toys and pornography and anything other than missionary position. I did not want to go into any sex store because I was concerned about being captured on those cameras and identified as someone who likes sex. *Oh no!* I was a good girl. My life was stable and under control and I liked it that way.

I did, however, flirt constantly with other men, especially under the influence of alcohol. I liked attention from men. I flirted with men, pushing the boundaries right up to the line and almost over it, and then I darted back to Tom for protection. I was completely sexually frustrated and did not know it.

When I turned 38, I went to a Slumber Party event. My friends encouraged me to go, and out of curiosity, I succumbed. "But I'm not getting anything," I told myself. A week later, my first vibrator arrived in the mail, and I experienced a clitoral orgasm for the first time. I was out of my mind with delight and constantly craving this experience. Pandora's Box was cracked open. I wanted to find out all of the ways I could get this rush, this heaven.

Suddenly I was questioning my sexual experiences, wondering if a clitoral orgasm felt this good, what did a vaginal orgasm feel like? Only one time with Tom had I experienced what I supposed was a squirting orgasm but it simply felt like I peed the bed. It was nothing like the sensations I was experiencing with the vibrator. Wow! I could not believe what I had missed.

It was exactly then in my sexual awakening that my cousin invited me to cross the line. Pandora's Box was wide open, and the lid was nowhere to be found.

☙

The affair begins.

Richard, my lover from Vegas, lives in New York and is married and has a daughter. We live so very far away from each other that we must carry on the affair with instant messenger, telephone and texting. I hear his voice and I am dripping with desire. He is afraid his wife will catch him in the act so I buy him a cellphone he can use at work to communicate with me.

I think I am being smart. I am having a virtual affair with a man who turns me on, who makes me feel wanted. But it is not without its challenges. I can only have Richard Monday through Friday during work hours. After work, I have no access to him. I have to endure the entire weekend without his attention, and it drives me crazy.

I spend most of my waking moments on nights and weekends living in a phantom memory in my head of lovemaking with Richard, and waiting out the silence until his voice returns. I love his voice with its deep baritone and New York accent. I want to feel this love all the time, all the time, all the time.

If Richard takes too long responding to my instant message, I am angry. I want his attention on call, on demand, to my schedule of need. And my need is very great indeed.

Controlling myself over the night and weekend is too much to bear already; during *my* time, I need his attention. Sometimes this becomes too much for Richard; it is suffocating. When he expresses this, I feel massive rejection and I spurn him for days. I lash out with angry words to hurt him as much as he has hurt me.

When I calm down I remember how good the love feeling is and I come crawling back, like a crack addict to his dealer, and Richard takes me back with stern warnings to behave myself like a good girl.

I promise to be Daddy's good girl.

ೞ

After one of these fights I decide to let Richard go because what I am doing feels wrong. I need to try to be a good wife. I need to be faithful. So I end it and tell Richard to return the phone.

The same day the mail comes, and my husband gets paperwork from the phone company and he discovers *my* extra phone after a little searching.

Now I am a two-time adulteress.

ೞ

I realize I am out of control. So I work extra hard at being a good wife and a good mother. I try to live without the love I so badly crave. I work with my therapist on controlling my urges, at understanding my behavior. I walk the straight and narrow. At least, I try to.

I run and run and run. The demons in my mind take longer to go dormant; now I run 10 miles, 12 miles, 15 miles before I find peace.

I am paying penance for my soul with my body.

ೞ

I talk to my therapist every week, and start to see that I am telling the same stories again and again with *fresh pain*. It is not getting better; it is getting worse. I am sick of myself and the story I tell. I simply want release from it. Everything is so hard.

It becomes harder when my husband decides to join my therapy sessions. Now I truly have no privacy. I am in lockdown even in therapy.

I am trying to work on having satisfying sex with my husband. I am allowing him to do things I never would allow before and I am trying to enjoy it. But it is so damn frustrating when it doesn't work the way it did with Richard. I don't know what to tell Tom to do to sexually please me. I don't understand my body and how it works. The only thing I know how to do is turn on my toy and let it do the work.

ନ୍ଧ

In contrast to my prison of therapy and home life, every art show gives me a sweet release with a new lover. In Nashville, a young gangsta freshly out of *real* prison. In Tennessee, a man I seduce at a bar. In Dallas, I have drunken sex with two men in one night: vanilla, then chocolate with a bout of puking and a cleansing bath in between. And there are men banging on the wall and the door to get in for Round 3. It has only been five months since I ended it with Richard, but the pace of affairs has been fast and furious.

I am desperate to recreate the rush and the satisfaction I had with Richard. The memory of it has become too distant and foggy to relive in my mind; I need it for real, in person. I confess each of these encounters to my husband; neither of us knows what to do to fix this, to save our marriage. We are just coping. Now when I come home from a trip, he just assumes the worst. He thinks maybe I need to do this, maybe I need to have this experimentation I never had in my twenties. Maybe I need to do it so I can move on.

I am out of control.
Plunging into the rabbit hole of my self-loathing.

I call Richard. He steps in to be my Daddy again. "Don't share Pinky with anyone… promise?" I promise. I don't want to end up with AIDS. I am beyond soap operas. When I confide in my girlfriend Collin now, I try to make light of it all, but I see real concern in her eyes. I am moving into a new dimension of depravity with these uncontrolled sexual urges.

What is wrong with me? Why can't I stop this?

ନ୍ଧ

The nightmares have returned. Over the course of my life, this nightmare has come at various times to plague me with terror. I enter some vintage-decorated room, in a mansion where people have lived for centuries, and usually there is a mirror or painting that I approach. As I look into it, the dread wells up inside, white noise swells inside my head in a crescendo of unbearable buzzing as I am gripped with panic that I will be consumed by whatever malignant entity has trapped me in this place. I can't scream to call for help. My voice is paralyzed. I am helpless and terrified until I am catapulted from my nightmare back into my bedroom. Usually, I must stay awake for at least 15 minutes; otherwise falling back to sleep simply descends me directly into the stranglehold of my invisible tormentor.

଼

I talk about how I feel to my therapist, to my close friends, and to myself in the mirror. I stare at myself in the mirror until I almost disappear and I wonder "Who is staring back at me?"

When I am staring at myself in the mirror, talking to myself about my heartbreak, I connect with myself, I really <u>see</u> myself, eyes welling up with tears, a woman in misery. Then ... I start to see something ... *bigger* than myself ... someone *wiser*, someone *older*. And this being comforts me with a deep knowing I feel inside.

It will get better. You are a good person.

଼

Richard is my secret weapon. He keeps me from sleeping with countless strangers. He keeps me, ironically, faithful to my husband. I am attempting to work things out with my husband, attempting to salvage our marriage. With Richard's help, I have put some structure into place to prevent me from sleeping with more men. He knows me well enough now to know when I am lying; he checks in with me regularly, reminding me of my promise to him. I am loyal to Richard, to my Daddy. I won't cheat.

My husband thinks maybe we need to spice things up as a couple, to embrace experimentation within the marriage; so we go to a local swingers club. We watch half a dozen people engage in an orgy. I kiss a woman because Tom thinks I should try it. We dance with others within eye shot. We even interview another couple as potential *partners*, over margaritas at Oasis by the lake; before they get there, we agree not to ask each other to take one for the team.

All of this feels wrong to me. My sexual needs, my deviant behavior, my *shame* can't stand the light of day of my marriage. It's like the train is riding just off the tracks. None of these things build intimacy between us; these things merely serve to widen the gap into a chasm.

I am afraid of where this chasm leads. If there is no safe place from these intense sexual needs, if there are no limits to its expression, I may be entirely consumed. I may be swept along a raging river that I am powerless to leave.

∞

I am so desperate for love: real, engaged love with a man, a man who doesn't ever want to *share* me. Everything that is happening is the opposite of what I feel I need; it is dark, twisted and <u>unfulfilling</u>. Everything we do is grasping at straws. We are trying to stop the ocean from washing away our castle built of sand.

Now when he tells me I am cooking the eggs wrong, I am angry.

I know I am wrong. I am not what Tom ever wanted. And I don't even know who I am.

But I am not *this*.

Suggestions

Awareness! Pay attention to your repeating patterns because they are the spotlight shining on your unhealed wound. When you notice a repeating pattern, hold yourself accountable by writing it down in your journal. Do not judge yourself for repeating the pattern. Merely seek to understand why you are repeating it. What is the underlying need that is unfulfilled? At this point in my story, the unfulfilled need is love. I do not feel love inside of me or from my marriage, so I am seeking it from men and romantic encounters outside of my marriage.

Acceptance! If a relationship is helping you to avoid destructive behaviors, it might be what you need right now, at this point in your journey, to keep putting one foot in front of the other. My relationship with Richard, as an "affair," would seem to be wrong. However, that relationship kept me in a secure space where I could refrain from causing further injury to myself while I sought to understand what was happening to me. Not all things in life fit into neat little boxes.

Gaze! There is something incredibly connective and healing that happens when you gaze at your reflection in the mirror. And I don't mean for 30 seconds. I mean for half an hour. Just simply witness yourself. I like to focus my gaze on one eye or the other and let my focus dissolve so that eventually I begin seeing all sorts of distorted visions of myself and eventually parts of me disappear from the reflection. Gazing at yourself allows you to drop into deep and loving contact with yourself. At first you may feel uncomfortable and exposed with nowhere to hide; this discomfort quickly dissipates when you accept it and surrender to the process.

Stop! Pay attention to how you feel in certain situations. If it doesn't feel right, don't do it. Period.

Quotes

"Holding on to anger is like grasping a hot coal with the intent of throwing it at someone else; you are the one who gets burned." — Buddha

"You do the work because the tests will continue to happen until we learn the lesson. There is one thing or theme that is following you in your life, frustrating you, haunting you, holding you back - own it, understand it, reach into the shadow and bring it to the light." — Chrispy Bhagat Singh[21]

"We don't see things as they are; we see them as we are." — Anaïs Nin

"I was no longer satisfied with being the walking dead, struggling through a life filled with stress, emptiness and fleeting moments of happiness. I felt that there had to be something more - another way- and I was determined to find it for myself." — Cecilia Zuniga[22]

"In oneself lies the whole world and if you know how to look and learn, the door is there and the key is in your hand. Nobody on earth can give you either the key or the door to open, except yourself." — Krishnamurti

"All the suffering and drama in your life is the result of what you have learned. Whatever you learn is alive. The image that you have of yourself is alive, and it lives in your mind. That image is not you, but it will use everything it perceives to justify its own existence. It is not you, but it is eating you alive and destroying your happiness." — Don Miguel Ruiz[23]

"If you take your happiness and put it in someone's hands, sooner or later, she is going to break it. If you give your happiness to someone else, she can always take it away." — Don Miguel Ruiz[24]

The Original Wound

I am seeing my therapist once a week. She tells me she is close to a diagnosis, but she needs more information from my early childhood.

Do I know if I was sexually or otherwise abused as a child? she asks. An inner knowing awakens, and I reveal my mother left my biological father because she said he was not good for me. Beyond that, she never told me why.

I met my father as an adult when I was in college and felt so very uncomfortable around him because of the way he would intensely stare right through me. He died of an AIDS-related illness in New York City before I was able to come to terms with my feelings about him and accept him into my life. Loving him was difficult on a primal level.

ॐ

When I am 14, I want to work a summer job but I need a social security number. For some reason, this is a huge deal to my mother and she is dragging her heels. I don't understand why she won't just help me. It's getting frustrating.

Finally, she sits me down and says. "We need to talk." I have that feeling like there is some huge invisible elephant in the room; I have had this feeling before.

My mother takes a deep breath. "Your Dad, Tom, is not your real father. I know you know this. But I told you that Fred was your father, and this is not true. He was your first step-father. Your real father is Jack Henderson."

There is a pause while I soak this in.

My mother continues. "Your Dad and I knew this moment would come, and if you want to meet your real father you can. I will arrange it. But you see, I have to tell you this now because you need your birth certificate to get your Social Security number, and your birth certificate lists your real father."

I let this soak in. It feels overwhelming. It feels like there is a huge unspoken truth.

I sense an immense shadow closing in, and I don't want to know the whole story right then. I am not ready.

"I just want my Social Security number. I'm not ready to meet him."

෴

When I am 18, I decide I want to meet my natural father. It is a curiosity always in the back of my mind. Who is this person? Am I like him? What do we have in common? Will meeting him change my life forever? Will meeting my father bring me peace and fulfillment and love? Is he the missing link?

My mother arranges through old family connections to find his current address. I write him a letter, with a return address that is a post office box in another town. There is excitement about this man; but it feels like protection is necessary, and I do not want to use my home address. My message in a bottle is tossed into the sea of the U.S. Postal Service.

He responds. He is ecstatic at the prospect of meeting me, of meeting his child.

He lives in New York City and at the time, we live in Connecticut so we arrange a visit to New York. I insist that my Dad and Mom go with me because while I am exhilarated and intensely curious about meeting Jack, I am afraid as well. I am afraid because he has been shrouded in mystery for my entire life.

I am on pins and needles all the way to New York City. I am close to throwing up at the prospect of meeting my natural father. The only thing that keeps me grounded is my safety blanket of Mom and Dad right there with me.

It is safe.

When we arrive at his apartment building in Manhattan, he buzzes us into the building. The ride in the elevator to his floor is excruciating, and several times I want to turn back. I clench my Mom's hand in my sweaty fist. I remind myself I am 18: a grown woman going to an Ivy League college. I am capable of this. I steel my nerves.

The doors to the elevator open and as we enter the darkened hallway I am confronted with him. His eyes glint and pierce through me like shards, and then I am in a stranglehold in his arms. I am shocked: I don't know what to do so I stand still while he grips me. He finally releases me, and I am grateful. I back up several feet and erect a barricade between us.

I do not want him in my space.

℃

Now nearly 42 years old, I am not surprised that I have to revisit the issue of my natural father, and that I have to finally dive into the shadows of Jack. I have felt this shadow calling my entire life, and I knew at some point, I would have to dance with it.

I invite my mother over to talk. I tell her I need to know about my early childhood, that my therapist needs to know my history in order to make a diagnosis and work toward my healing. This request alerts my mom that something bad is going on with me. She knows I am in therapy, and have been very up and down lately. A mother knows when her child is in pain.

My mom and I sit at my dining room table, and she tells me "I never wanted to taint your view of your father when you met him, and that's why I never told you." She then says that she heard him talking to me as a baby several times and saying he was going to teach me how to please a man, how to get a man to do anything I want. Eyes filled with tears she tells me that she walked in on him giving me a bath, but he was naked in the tub with me. I was sitting on his lap. She says she took me away from him before he could do any harm to me.

She tells me she never thought she could get pregnant. She married my father knowing he had been emotionally abused as a child, had witnessed his mother having sex with countless men, was abandoned outside hotel rooms, and was in every way imaginable, neglected. He was not suitable material for fatherhood. She did not think having a child was a possibility for her because the doctors told her she could not get pregnant. But then, the doctors were proven wrong and she was blessed with me.

As soon as she realized he was intending to express himself sexually with me when I was just over a year old, she got me away from him. At the time, the courts wanted proof that he was sexually abusing me. My mother would not wait for the abuse to be recorded, because that meant allowing the abuse to happen to me. So she divorced him and remarried a man who eventually moved her far away to the Northeast. We spent 2 years in visitation with my natural father, until I was 3 years old, before we moved.

Living with my first step-father was jumping straight into the fire. During the few years we lived with him, he was physically and emotionally abusive to my mother, and although I do not remember it, my mother tells me I witnessed the abuse, including several fist fights with my natural father and the time he tried to throw my mother off a second-story balcony at our apartment. I remember my first memory: my stepfather's hand coming down at my face to punish me for touching his guitar when he left the room. I was three years old.

My mother tells me of how she got me into therapy right away after leaving my father, and during the time we were living with the abusive step-father. She tells me I was biting my arms, and leaving red welting bite marks; I was two to three years old during the time I saw this therapist. Pictures of me reveal a frightened little girl with dark circles under her eyes.

I was a shadow girl.

ભ

Once my mother reveals my history, she needs to know why am I asking? What is wrong? Why have I been so sad? She has theories, and I dismiss them. But she is persistent, and finally, I tell her what has happened.

She is so saddened by this revelation, and feels tremendous responsibility for creating the environment in which I have been wounded. I tell her that she rescued me before I was really abused, and that takes courage; more courage than many mothers can muster.

I am grateful to her.
She did everything she could to rescue me.
This is my story.
It is what it is.

❧

I tell my therapist about what my mother said about my childhood, and she gives me the diagnosis: Borderline Personality Disorder (BPD). Looking this up on Wikipedia I see how true this is. I can agree with the majority of statements made in this article about my condition. Intellectually, I see I can be classified by this diagnosis. I can cognitively understand why I am the way I am, why I have behaved the way I have behaved.

But how can something *I don't even remember* have shaped my existence?

❧

I am working hard at understanding my diagnosis, and in many ways it is giving me compassion for myself and my wounds. It is also, however, giving me permission for my uncontrolled outbursts and erratic behavior. I am working so hard at therapy and controlling myself and suppressing my urges, but then I indulge myself in self-pity and feel rebellious and so I swing the other direction into self-destructive behaviors.

I don't understand myself at all. I feel like a foreigner to my own experience. I have been labeled by a diagnosis that is ominous and condemning, and as I review my life, I see the signposts of this disorder illuminating the choices I made at every step.

I don't want to be identified with BPD; I don't want to be defined by it. I resent this diagnosis. I resent the trap it puts me into, like I will never be free of this label. It feels like a black mark on my scholastic record; it feels like I got an F in the school of life. I am not perfect. And with this label tattooed on my forehead, I never will be.

I want to pretend that all of this never happened. But then I slip into self-destructive behavior and because I have a dawning awareness, I am freshly confronted with my truth: I am broken.

My whole life I have worked so hard to be perfect, and now I find out that I've been scarred and slated for imperfection right from the start. My perfect record is blemished. My perfect life is a lie.

A cacophony bangs around in my head and heart as I process this new awareness while I negotiate daily life in my marriage. All of this is more than I can bear. I want out. I want quiet.

൪

The nightmare has returned, and this time it culminates in a hateful shrew that bellows:

I hate you, Hate You, HATE YOU!!!

I am flung from my nightmare into waking terror. My heart pounds as if it will burst right through my ribs.

I am terrified to go back to sleep.

൪

Suggestions

Dance with Shadow! One of the hardest things to do is to square your shoulders and walk headfirst into your own shadows. Your shadow is innately more frightening than anyone else's shadow. You know best what scares you most, and therefore are able to concoct your own worst nightmare. Stepping into your shadow takes a measure of faith that you will survive the experience. I visualize Indiana Jones[25] taking the leap of faith across the bottomless crevice.

Pamper Yourself! Dancing with shadows, delving in the darkness of our own psyches, is hard work. Comfort yourself with massages to relax and restore your physical, mental, and emotional bodies. When we get professional bodywork, the massage therapist works out knots in our muscles, and also releases toxins trapped in our tissues. Consider using a massage therapist who can also perform energy work, such as Reiki[26]. Energy work is restorative: it releases blocks and toxins, and helps the flow of energy through our bodies. And it feels really _good_.

Ask for Help! I never liked asking for help because I felt it made me weak, and it made me dependent on others. However, through the spiritual journey that has been my path during the last several years, I have realized that being vulnerable enough to ask for help is a sign of tremendous strength. It actually speaks to your faith in yourself that one day you will be able to return the favor. So ask for help. Because when you are healed, you will be of vastly greater service in this world. Trust that you have a great deal to offer others.

Seek to Understand, But Don't Get Lost in the Story!
Psychotherapy is wonderful in its scientific capacity for classifying a wide range of mental and emotional human ailments. But a diagnosis is only a one-dimensional attempt at putting a living, breathing three-dimensional being into a tidy little box to store on a shelf. Your humanity, your soul, demands that you understand where you have been, and the forces that brought you to where you are standing today. You then take that knowledge and TRANSFORM into the Self you wish to become.

Quotes

"I've learned that this is how it works: once you make the commitment to 'seek,' everything that is in your way on that yellow brick road comes forth for clearing, so you can move beyond it. And, everything you need to support you on the journey also comes forth. There's no turning back; you have no choice but to keep going. Well, that's not exactly true. You always have choice. The thing is, if you stop, it's like standing in the middle of the fires of change; and if you go back, you return to a life of self-denial and lies, only they feel bigger now because you've gotten a glimpse of the truth." — Cecilia Zuniga[27]

"If we can share our story with someone who responds with empathy and understanding, shame can't survive." — Brené Brown[28]

"Embrace the story to learn its lessons. And now…lose it and write a new one." — Kerri Hummingbird Lawnsby

"Although your mind resists it, the fact is that you have a choice between having the life you want or having the reasons you can't have that life. You can have joy and peace, or you can have that big black bag full of all the sorrowful incidents and accidents that happened to you in your childhood or in your last relationship. You can have your wounds or you can have your glory. You can live the life of a victim, burdened by the traumas of your past, or you can live the life of a hero, but you can't do both. If you want to feel empowered, you need to make a conscious decision to dream a sacred dream and practice courage."
— Alberto Villoldo, PhD[29]

"Be you, with you. That is the practice and I suggest, the Magic. You, done for you, by you, in you. You are the alchemist, the White Witch, Wizard or Warlock, the one who comes to the experience with the desire to know self, and to refine experience." — Chrispy Bhagat Singh[30]

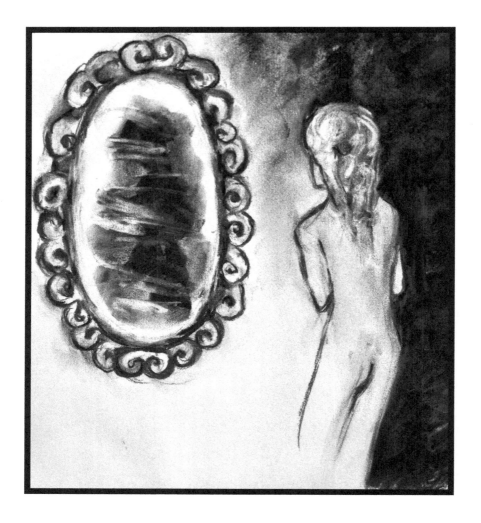

Adopting Fearlessness

But if I get off my knees
I might recall
I'm 20 feet tall [31]

I have discovered the rope has an end. Tom knows something in me has changed. Like a vulture, he circles around and around me, peering at my computer screen behind my back, checking my phone every time it beeps. "Who is he?" he asks. "No one," I say.

In fact, it is not a he. It is a she. It is me.

I choose me. I am leaving my marriage because what is on the other side has got to be better. Because after three years it has not gotten better; it has gotten worse. I don't know what has happened with us to make this chain of events over the past few years possible. I don't understand how we went from our fairytale wedding on the cliff overlooking Kapalua Bay in Maui to the affair that started the downward spiral of disconnection and distrust and despair that has led me to this moment where I am choosing to walk away from my best friend.

What I know is that there is a huge gap between then and now, and in the middle is a chasm filled with self-judgment, disappointment, anger, blame, guilt, and loathing, and I am drowning in it. I can't fulfill the perfect vision of wife that I held in my heart and mind when I took my marriage vows because I am clearly, radically, imperfect. I can't face how far I have fallen from grace. I can't accept myself and my choices. I don't know how to keep living in this marriage.

I feel like I am living in a prison from which I desperately want to be free. I don't know who I am anymore. I don't know how to stop feeling angry and defiant, how to stop feeling judgment and blame, how to stop myself from rebelling against this marriage. I don't know how to cope with my behavior, with all of the things I've done against myself and against my husband.

I understand why my husband has tightened the noose over the last couple of years, but his control is strangling me.

Inside, I am chaos. My foundation has been up-ended with the discovery of my psychological diagnosis, and I do not know what this means about *me*. From where I am today, I don't know how to do anything but start swimming. This marriage has become an anchor binding me to my despair; I must be free of it or I will drown.

I have the cool abstract awareness of a person who has just survived a car wreck. This is simply the most logical next step.

The "car" is totaled.

It's time to salvage what there is left of my friendship with my husband before that is exhausted as well. It's time to part ways so that we can work together to raise our sons. It's time to let go before we hate each other.

I review my finances for the past year and determine I will have enough income to survive.

◌

I am instantly relieved. The marriage, my marriage, is over. A weight has been lifted off my chest. I feel free and almost joyful. After stuffing my belongings into my minivan and driving them load-by-load to my new rented home, I have moved into the first home I have ever had in my adult life that was simply mine.

My sofa. My chair. My television. My bed. My brand new sheets never before used by him. My towels. Mine. Mine. Mine.

From the first night in my home, I take a bubble bath every night while sipping wine by candlelight.

This must be how the butterfly feels
when it breaks free and stretches its wings
for the first time...
aching limbs from being bound,
but excitement about flying.

Life continues as before, yet far less complicated. I have left behind the bag of painful memories of all the times I betrayed my marriage vows. Without the pressure of trying to control my desires, to fit into my "half" of the couple-body, there is freedom and relief from my critical inner judge.

I date a couple of men; I have a dozen others on text. I enjoy the constant attention. I enjoy the freedom of choosing when I want to invite a man into my world, when I want to invite a man to my bed. I enjoy that I can make the man leave. "Goodbye!"

Most of all, I enjoy the peace and quiet. I enjoy the mental space and clarity. I enjoy the simplicity of living for myself. I stop seeing my therapist because I'm tired of talking. I turn off the television and the radio. I am tired of noise.

I have stopped scratching my neck.

∽

My husband tries to kiss me when he drops off the kids. I allow it; I allow him to discover for himself that it is over between us. He agrees to the divorce. We begin the paperwork.

I cook scrambled eggs: the way I like to cook them, with my spatula and my pan. My eggs taste good. They are definitely *not* burned.

∽

I am drowning in paperwork. My husband and I communicate almost as much now as we did before we were separated. *Is this the way it will be?* At least I can turn off my phone. I set a special tone for his text messages, so I know I can ignore them (or at least not get excited it is someone else). Then I set his messages to silent. It is such blissful freedom to set this boundary.

He wants the wooden dining table and leather-backed chairs from Restoration Hardware. I want the minivan. We stake our claims on the bounty from our marriage. We put it all in writing. Even the dog has a line item.

∽

My heart's deepest desire has not changed. Even with moving to a new home and all the transitions of divorce and managing the children's schedules between two locations my focus is still on FINDING LOVE.

I sign onto a dating site and start crafting the story that I share with prospective dates. I put my message in a bottle to the Universe, and it answers ... with **Z**!

I am absolutely smitten with this man. YES! This is what I want Universe! YES, YES, YES!

Only he lives in Atlanta, which is really ok for now because I need to heal and live on my own for a while. But isn't it great that he is there and I found him so when I'm ready it will all magically materialize into the happy ending I always believed would be possible? *Sigh.*

I concentrate on him while taking my bubble bath, and send out heart waves of love through the Universe to gain his attention and magically he texts me! Time and time again. It is an exciting time filled with possibilities.

Z is so witty and clever and funny. Every time he texts me he has a new nickname for me.

"How's my Pinka-potamus?"
"Hey..Pinkalicious! What's up?"
"Pinka-Saurus! Are you grumpy today?"

I ask him how many nicknames can he come up with? And he says *infinity*. I believe him. I love how fun it is to converse with this man, to play with words, to tease and entice.

I delight in the silly quirky side of Z, but it's the serious side of him that is making me fall in love with this man. He has walked this path of divorce and independence before me and he has learned a great deal on his own journey of self-discovery.

Every time we talk I feel as if I have only tapped the surface of a deep ocean of wisdom, and I want to soak it up. And as I am soaking up his wisdom, I also want to bask in the glow of his attention which feels like sunshine to me. I want to be invited into his secret Z Society as a Top Agent and No. 1 Confidante.

Pinky Pea and Hunny Z…for Infinity!

଼

My children come home from school crying after two days with Tom. Tom has a girlfriend and they have seen him kiss her. It has only been two months since I moved out. They are heartbroken. I am caught off guard, not knowing how to respond. I hug them. I tell them I am sorry. The earth under my feet is suddenly missing. I realize I am alone. Completely alone. I feel sudden panic: what do I do about this situation? What can I do?

I call Z and he listens. But then he says "Kerri, this is too much for a new relationship. You're going to have to talk to your friends, spread this around. Don't you have friends you can call?"

I really feel alone now.

The children go to bed and I drink wine and I pace frantically up and down through the kitchen. Panic swells inside my chest and my breath goes shallow as I start to cry. I want to flee but where would I go? I want to escape this feeling because to linger here…to linger in this moment…is to allow myself to feel sorrow that my children are hurting because of my choices. I collapse crying on my bed. I cry until there are no more tears, and I fall asleep.

The next morning, my older son brings me the sweetest salvation from the lips of babes. "Mommy, don't worry about us. You did the right thing. You had to leave. It's hard for us right now, but it will get better. And you're so much happier now." I want to cry, this time out of gratitude: somehow I have raised the most wonderful son in the world.

I realize something significant. I have no control over anything outside the four walls of my home. This brings me peace because it means I can let go of everything else. I think of Stephen Covey[32] and his spheres of influence. I realize mine is a rectangle called my house, and a circle made from my arms embracing my children.

I feel the earth under my feet. For the first time in my life I have the awareness that I can be my own security, my own rock, my own sacred tree. Tiny roots extend downward from my feet, exploring the earth's surface, grounding me as I learn how to extend my branches out and up.

∾

The joy of being alone is starting to wane. I constantly feel like something is missing. Did I leave something out of place? And eventually, I realize, I miss having 'the other half.'

From 15 hours away by car, and 4 hours by plane, Z tells me, "Kerri, it's like you're trying to find a replacement for your ex. Like you want a guy to just step in and resume where you left off. It doesn't work like that."

I resent that he is right. I did just think I would walk out of my marriage and instantly find true love. I was that naive and ridiculous. And now what? How long does this part last?

Until you're healed.

What the fuck does that mean?

∾

For years I have run marathons to flee it.
I have consumed vast quantities of
alcohol to numb myself to it.
I have kept moving, moving, moving.
Today I stand still and let it catch up to me.
And I am saturated by it.
Crushed by the enormous weight of it.
But there is hope...My heart is still beating.

One day it catches up to me that the journey I set out on when I was 22 has come to an end. And it didn't end the way I thought it would. In fact, I lived in a fantasy for a good long time while pretending I was living the life I had envisioned. I don't know when I shifted from living in love to pretending to live in love, but I know when I woke up from the dream.

It was the day I realized I loved someone else, and that the love I felt was a foreign feeling.

∞

Our house sells. The home we renovated together and spent all our savings on because we were going to live there until the children were grown. Ha!

It is the dirty, stick-to-it part of the divorce. Clean up your act, move your stuff, remove all traces of you from the house. Let the dream go. Let the story go. It's over.

I say good-bye to the beautiful studio made just for me so I could create artwork. I am deeply, profoundly, and utterly devastated to leave my studio. My studio. No longer mine. All that effort in designing and building our dream home and studio where we could live happily ever after, and it is going to be enjoyed by someone else. My path lies elsewhere.

Turning down a different road.
An unknown road with a mystery destination
and no one to walk it with me.

∞

My life almost ends in an instant. A pickup truck pulls out into the intersection where I am driving 40mph. There is no time to stop. Barely time to think "Brakes!" I see his face and I pray I am not ending someone's life. My prayer is answered and everyone survives unscathed, including Daddy Dawg who was riding shotgun and should have been flung through the front window. He is my lifeboat. I cannot live without that little dog.

Daddy Dawg cuddles with me in bed every night. He is warmth and comfort. When he jumps sideways he makes me burst into laughter. When he licks my neck and face I giggle. Some benevolent force spares his little life for me.

The minivan I won in the divorce is wrecked. The old life is done.

I am reborn. I am filled with gratitude for the many blessings I do have in my life. I am uncertain where my path is taking me, but I am so glad I have my children and my dog. I cuddle my little dog, my new man, as I walk on.

℞

There are days I do not leave my bed. Working for myself as a consultant affords me this luxury; or, otherwise stated, lets me fully immerse in my depression. All the change in my life is taking its toll on me. My steam has run out, and I spend days without muster. I get the kids to school late even though the school is only 10 minutes away. I leave the blinds drawn. I am in a chrysalis state in my cocoon. I am comfortable in my shadowy home, snuggled in my bed, spooning with faithful Daddy Dawg.

I drink wine, a bottle a night. I take baths. I scour the Internet dating sites for men to give me attention. I still talk to Z but it is not progressing and I feel frustrated by his common sense and reserve.

Plunge in with me!! I want joy and love...Now!

But he only says "I hear you talking. We shall see." I begin to really despise hearing that. I am like a crack addict. I need a fix to keep moving. My need for affection is so great, and he is miserly in his distribution.

℞

I have no interest in disciplining my children. My inner child has emerged and she is resentful of authority; she likes to do what she wants, and she is perfectly fine letting my children do what they want too. Some days the three of us just cuddle together on my bed, waking up slow and late on a Sunday morning, hugging each other and saying lots of "I love you."

I play video games with my children and they laugh heartily at me because I can't get through doorways in *Left 4 Dead* (which Z has taught me to play) and the zombies are coming, and I am shrieking and giggling as I fall off the plank and down two stories where zombies consume me whole because I don't know how to work the darned controller. I am a hopeless *noob*.

I am restless being at home, but I don't have the energy or desire to have friends over. I make a habit of going to the local neighborhood bar to eat dinner and drink fancy cocktails. I flirt with the bartender who is twenty years younger; I humor myself there is a chance he finds me attractive.

∞

I am going to the chiropractor because my back is hurting, my neck is stiff, and I just feel tight everywhere. My chiropractor takes x-rays of my spine and shows me how out of alignment I am. He tells me how spinal misalignment can choke your spinal cord, disrupting the lifeline of communication between your body and your brain. He tells me that subluxations, or the misalignment, can be caused by physical or emotional trauma to the body (injuries, stress, depression, toxins). I know exactly what traumas my spinal cord has experienced: my divorce and my car accident.

Most weeks, spinal corrections are improving my posture and my level of pain. But some weeks, the tough weeks, my doctor notices that corrections are not as effective. Because I am wearing my heart on my sleeve these days, he sees my depression. He gently tells me I need to work on healing the emotional burdens. Healing emotional pain is sometimes the only thing that will take care of a problem when everything else has been tried and has failed. My doctor hugs me; I am grateful for his empathy.

∞

Twenty years of a relationship with my best friend for most of my life ends in a courtroom. He doesn't come: I stand alone before the judge.

I am free. I am alone. A chapter of my life has ended. Another chapter has begun. There is space, and time, and vastness, and emptiness. I am thankful there has been no drama with our parting; I am thankful my ex-husband has been a gentleman. It could have been different; it could have been much more painful.

I don't know how to feel on this particular day. How should I feel upon ending a relationship that grew me from a 22 year old baby into a mature woman and mother? How should I feel upon reflection of all the sacred moments we shared on our way to adulthood?

ᙢ

I am sunbathing at the beach on the morning
I become a wife. The breeze brushes past,
cooling sun-soaked skin. With eyes closed,
I hear the waves crashing into shore, and
I savor my last moments as a girl.

ᙢ

I don't know where I'm going
I barely know where I've been
I've been searching and searching
Never feeling content
I've been running and running
Keeping my eyes closed
I guess I'll finally stand still
And let that flower grow…

—*Kerri Hummingbird Lawnsby*
Spring 2011

Suggestions

Patience! Anyone who knows me is laughing right now at reading this advice because I am notoriously impatient. What I have learned, however, is that doing nothing can be extremely healing after you have been through turmoil in your life. Allow time and space for doing nothing. Embracing rest and reflection and quiet creates the space to discover what we need to let go of. Be patient about progress and change and the arrival of all the things you want in your life; those things will come. But life is a process, and you can't skip over the steps or speed it up. (Believe me, I tried.)

More Pampering! If you have just made a major transition in your life like ending a relationship or moving, now is absolutely the time to pamper yourself like a baby. My nightly ritual of bubble baths by candlelight began at this point in my life and has not ended yet. I now use my bath time to relax, sip wine, and listen to spiritual wisdom from audio casts. I also continue to indulge in massage and Reiki energy work, at least monthly, because it is healing and helps my body to move the energy.

Unconditional Love! Keep the love flowing in your heart by giving it unconditionally to a pet or your children, or anyone in your life that you can love with reckless abandon. I found it immensely healing to love on Daddy Dawg and my boys; as much love as I gave, I received back and then some! Love feels wonderful when you are hurting inside.

Trust Your Process! It is natural for self-doubt to enter our hearts any time we make a major shift in our lives. Our ego mind has an important job: to protect us from harm. Making a major life change puts us in the space of the unknown which can trigger fear; fear activates our ego mind as protector. Our ego mind remembers all the ways we got hurt in the past, and reminds us of those things constantly. It also attempts to anticipate new sources of pain, and alert us with what HeatherAsh Amara calls "disaster mind." [33] Give yourself peace when these thoughts arise by breathing deep, exhaling slowly, and creating a mental pause while you focus on your breath. In the tiny silence created by this practice, remind yourself to trust YOU.

Quotes

"Change is not linear but a never-ending spiral process of inspiration, fruition, deepening, death, and rebirth… With the more recent ability to communicate … with one another via email and cell phones, you might believe that internal transformation or external change should happen this instant. The result of this kind of mental pressure is frustration, self-judgment, and confusion." — HeatherAsh Amara[34]

"You have a limit to the amount of abuse you will accept, but no one in the world abuses you more than you abuse yourself. The limit of your self-abuse is the limit you will tolerate from other people. If someone abuses you more than you abuse yourself, you walk away, you run, you escape. But if someone abuses you a little less than you abuse yourself, perhaps you stay longer. You still deserve that abuse." — Don Miguel Ruiz[35]

"Every great and deep difficulty bears in itself its own solution. It forces us to change our thinking in order to find it." — Niels Bohr

"Authenticity is a collection of choices that we have to make every day. It's about the choice to show up and be real. The choice to be honest. The choice to let our true selves be seen." — Brené Brown[36]

"One aspect of who we were is dying and out of the imaginal selves emerges someone new. We are moving from good to great, we are moving from caterpillar to butterfly, we are moving from who we used to be to who we can be." — Marianne Williamson, 2009

"I say that we are more like snakes than butterflies: we shed our skins over and over and over again during a lifetime, going deeper and deeper into ourselves each time, letting the old go and birthing new parts of who we are in the moment." — Cecilia Zuniga[37]

"The soft always overcomes the hard—the roundest drop of softest water will wear away the toughest block of granite, given its three warriors: time, patience and perseverance." — Chrispy Bhagat Singh[38]

There is a jewel lotus flower unfolding deep within my soul.

Embracing Spirituality

The fire walk stretches before me.
I have taken the first few steps with confidence
in my face and trepidation in my heart. My feet are burning. But I will not
turn back. My true self awaits me at the other side.

♥

When we are ready for transformation, a teacher appears to point us to the doorway that leads into a different reality. For me, that teacher is Gina. Gina has become my parent's step-daughter during my transition from married to single, while I have been lost in my shadows. She rents the guest house on their property, watches their dogs when they leave town, eats dinner with them, and spends countless hours talking with them.

When I begin to emerge from my cocoon, I finally notice her. *Who is this?* I wonder. Witnessing her interactions with my mother one afternoon I am suddenly aware that things have shifted in my world while I was asleep. I feel a pang of jealousy at the depth of her relationship with my mother and father. At the same time, I feel gratitude. It is a perplexing duality.

Gina has led a different life from my own. Over the last 10 years, she has been single while she raised her daughter, now grown and in her twenties. She has walked a path that is very similar to the one I am awakening to: the path of motherhood. The path of Self. The path of solitude.

I admire her, and I want to avoid her, all at the same time. I realize I am afraid of what she represents: I do not want to be alone. And 10 years is a life sentence from where I stand.

☙

I choose to embrace my fear and accept an invitation from Gina to go to yoga. I've never done yoga, but I have always had the habit of stretching out on the floor in an array of postures, much to the amusement of friends as far back as my college roommates, so I figure this might be something I would like.

In fact, I do. I discover that focusing on my breath quiets the churning in my mind and brings me peace. Moving my body to my breath activates a deep sense of reverence for my Self and my body.

Partly, this is because I am listening to the wisdom emerging from Chrispy, my yoga instructor, during Vinyasa. With his long hair pulled up into a bun, Chrispy strides like a matador across the room, bellowing challenges to his students to hold the posture longer, face your shadow, stay in the present because the past and the future are only shadows of your mind. I am in *The Matrix* in a yoga studio, and it is fascinating and wonderful.

∞

I find I want to confide in Gina. I want her wisdom to enter my life, to help me navigate these uncharted waters that, quite honestly, frighten me. She invites me to dinner and I accept. It is somewhat strange to drive to my parents' house and pass their driveway to enter hers, to see their house from her home. I have that independent feeling like I had when I had just graduated college and visited a friend at her apartment.

At this time in my life, I am making a mess of things with Z. Let's face it, I am messy and I am spilling out all over the place emotionally.

I tell Gina the story of what is happening with Z, how much I feel for him and how he keeps pushing me away, and how I keep messing things up anew. She listens, and then she asks me if I want to try something. *Yes! Anything!*

So Gina goes into the other room and comes back to the dining table with a little grey bag. She tells me to concentrate on a question and then pick three little tiles out of the bag and lay them down. My question is something like: "Will Z and I ever be together?" She looks at the tiles I have laid down and starts to read from her book. I really don't like what I am hearing because it is telling me things like:

The winter of the spiritual life is upon you. You may find yourself entangled in a situation to whose implications you are, in effect, blind.

And:

Be aware that no quick results can be expected. A span of time is usually involved; hence the key words "One Year," symbolizing a full cycle before the reaping, the harvest or deliverance.[39]

One YEAR??? Hell no! But in my heart, I know these little tiles have spoken truth. In fact, it's kind of scary how closely the meaning attributed to those little tiles resembles my current circumstances.

Gina witnesses my struggle over this prediction, and she has compassion for it. She asks me if I would like to try something else. I am willing, so she asks me to gaze into her eyes and say "I love myself." Repeat it over and over again until you believe it, she encourages.

I gaze into her eyes and open my mouth to speak, but suddenly I have a lump in my throat. I clear my throat and begin to speak, and as I say the words "I love myself," I feel my bravado slipping through my fingers like sand; my face reddens and my eyes well up with tears. I maintain eye contact with Gina, and with her as my witness, I say it again and again, and now I am openly weeping. Gina holds space for me as I explore this deepest vulnerability. And when the panic and the tears have subsided, there is a peaceful calm.

We hug. I am grateful for this experience, and for this friendship.

෬

For at least six months I have avoided psychotherapy, and I really do not want to return to it. But, I do feel the need for guidance to help me walk this new path.

As I sit waiting for yoga to begin one day, I am inspired by a notion: what if I ask Chrispy to be my spiritual mentor? Would he do it? I mean, he seems like he really knows his shit. I lean over and whisper to Gina. It turns out she has just been looking at his bio and knows that he offers "spiritual counseling." I have no idea what this is, but it sounds good.

I stand up and walk over to Chrispy and I say, "I have no idea what spiritual counseling is, but I hear that you offer it, and I want to try it."

"Great!" he says. "Talk to me after class."

ය

The first time we meet, Chrispy is interviewing me to see what kinds of demons I am facing; he needs to determine if he can help me or not. So I give him the rough outline of my sordid past, and talk about my hopes for healing and moving forward into a new life. He bites. I am enthused because this means he thinks he can help me. Relief washes over me.

ය

A week later Chrispy and I meet for our first session and it is not a moment too soon. I have had another argument with Z and I am dying to lay it on the table for Chrispy. I explain in detail all the reasons why I am so hurt and offended by Z's actions and inactions and words, and I am crying and wounded and a victim.

Chrispy pauses, looks me in the eye, places his hands on the table, rotates them 180° like he is spinning a platter from facing him to facing me, and turns my entire world inside out:

You did this.

In a lifetime of therapy, no one ever stopped me and held me accountable for the role I played in my own life. No one ever made me see how I was creating my own reality—until I met this man with hair down to his hips.

Gulp.

ය

I try rectifying things with Z, and momentarily the reconciliation is successful, but by the next time I see Chrispy, I have visited Z and it was too much for me. Being in his home, in his *space*, has overwhelmed me and I have acted out because I am in love with him. I spent the entire weekend challenging him instead of *being* with him. In fact, I forced a revelation from him that he said "I love you" before he meant it. He wants a month of silence and space. I am completely distraught.

Chrispy tells me to go into a closet and face my shadow: what does it mean if Z does not love me?

It means that I am not worthy of the love of someone I hold in high regard. It means that I am deficient.... too emotionally complicated....or too irritating, or too needy or too clingy, or unworthy of a love from a special person. It means I am not attractive enough, stylish enough, pretty enough in face and body. It means I have a deficiency marking me as sub-par. It means I am not worthy of love that is un-coerced.

If Z sees me for who I truly am, he will not like what he sees. And if someone special like Z does not like what I am...then what?

Z does not need me; his life is not lacking happiness, his desires do not drive him. He is thoughtful, measured, careful of his space and emotional happiness, caring of himself.

What can I possibly add to his life to make my presence there worthwhile? Why would anyone with a happy existence choose to be with a person like me?

A person who <u>complicates</u> existence?

What happens now that I have realized my problems are of my own making? That I have let my own fears potentially destroy what I hold dear? If I don't get my shit together I will never have the love I seek. Apology rendered to Z. And now to face myself.

෴

I face myself in the mirror with my hand on my heart and said these words until I stop crying and start believing:

"There is worth here."

I am lost in the winter of my soul. The snow flurries are so thick I cannot find my way home alone. But I promise myself, spring is coming.

ଔ

I am wrapping my mind around three weeks with no contact with Z. I am going insane minute by minute. Watching the hockey game with my kids I am seriously having trouble staying in the moment. I am using some of the yoga techniques Chrispy taught me to remind myself to return to the moment: *keep focusing on the puck*! Staying in the moment is hard work; I am uncomfortable in my own skin.

I go into the closet and sit with my fear, with my shadow. I sit with the reality that this special relationship may very well be over because I do not yet understand how to handle myself with the love emotion and my compulsive need for it.

In the closet, I create a mantra which brings me some measure of peace for the time being.

I am the love that I seek.
I am the light that I seek.
The love and the light are inside ME.

In between this mantra, I tell myself:

I do not need love because I am made of it.

ଔ

I realize there is healing to be done with the relationship with my ex-husband, and I am ready to do it. I write by hand 160 well-intentioned statements of gratitude in a journal for the man who was my best friend and soul mate for 20 years. It takes me several weeks and a lot of focus to conceive of meaningful thanks that I can share with all my heart. I give him this gift on his 45th birthday. It feels good to witness and honor my history with this man: no longer my husband, but hopefully my friend for life.

Simultaneous with crafting all of this gratitude, Gina suggests I try Reiki energy work, so my chiropractor gives me a reference and I book an appointment. I learn from Kat, my Reiki energy healer, that to move forward in my life I need to sever my connection with my ex-husband energetically, and reclaim that energy for my own healing; it's a process called *Cutting the Cords*. During our session, she massages me until I am relaxed and ready for this energetic release, and then we do the visualization.

She tells me to visualize my ex-husband out there in the world, and then to visualize long braided cords of different colors extending from my body to his along my chakras, or energy points in my body. Seven chakras from the top of my head to my sit-bone: seven cords that bind. One by one, I visualize a giant pair of scissors cutting the cord that binds me to him from each chakra, releasing him and retracting my energy back into myself, and as I cut the cords I forcefully *HUFF* all the air out of my diaphragm. As I release him, I feel gratitude for all that we shared in our life together and peaceful acceptance for where we are today.

଼

I continue to struggle with the absence of Z. It occurs to me that love bestowed upon the wrong person is like pouring water on sand in the vast desert. At some point, I decide I would rather pour my water on fertile ground and see what garden emerges, and so I log back into the dating site and cast my baited hook into the river of life. At yoga, my instructor shares this quote, and I feel as if it is a message to try again.

> *"If you're really listening, if you're awake to the poignant beauty of the world, your heart breaks regularly. In fact, your heart is made to break. Its purpose is to burst open again and again, so that it can hold ever more wonder." —Andrew Harvey*

଼

I am heartbroken that things have not worked out with Z, but at the same time I know I must move forward without regrets. I ask Chrispy for advice on how to leave my feelings behind.

Chrispy tells me of an ancient tradition whereby women cleanse their auras by splashing water from the river, washing past relationships out of the aura that rises from shoulders in an arc above their heads.

At home that night, I fill my tub with a warm Epsom salt bath, and I meditate with eyes closed as I splash water over my head, visualizing it cleansing the energetic rainbow connecting my shoulders. As I do this, I am amazed that each splash of water brings a new remembrance of a past boyfriend or lover. With each memory, I hold the vision and I forgive and release that experience into my past with a prayer:

I'm sorry. Please forgive me. I love you. Thank you.

The bath-time meditation goes on for hours, and when I am done, I marvel at the water all around my bathroom floor.

I feel lighter and freer.

 C₿

I buy myself a set of Runes, which are the little tiles Gina shared with me. I decide to consult the oracle about my destiny on a more frequent basis; to check in, so to speak. For many weeks, I pull the same tiles out of the bag, and I simply do not understand how this can be possible. This is either a trick or I am stuck.

And then one day at yoga, during Shivasana meditation, I have a vision of myself at 22. I witness my loneliness and insecurity, and I travel back through time as a comforting spirit to this younger version of me, to this troubled heart. I feel like some small measure of healing has taken place, and I am immensely grateful.

This evening, I pull out my Runes and draw *new* tiles! I am ecstatic! The tiles tell me I have reached a Breakthrough, a Transformation Day:

Drawing Dagaz often signals a major shift or breakthrough in the process of self-change, a complete transformation in attitude, a 180-degree turn. For some, the transition is so radical that they are no longer able to live the ordinary life in the ordinary way... In each life there comes at least one moment which, if recognized and seized, transforms the course of that life forever. Rely, therefore, on radical trust, even though the moment may call for you to leap empty-handed into the void. With this Rune your Warrior Nature reveals itself.[40]

I dance and jump around the room in my joy!

ଔ

At dinner one evening around this time, Gina mentions how she was deeply healed by a friend of hers who is a Shaman. I have no idea what this is, but make a mental note. Later that evening, when I return home, I do an Internet search and find a local Shaman, Gerry Starnes. Not only that, he is about to begin a six month intensive and experiential exploration of contemporary shamanic wisdom for living authentically called *Spirit Paths*.

Spirit is winking at me.

My Warrior Nature revealed, I request to be interviewed to participate in this experience!

ଔ

When I arrive at Gerry's office, I take a seat in the waiting area which looks like someone's down-home living room. He greets me and invites me to his office where I remove my shoes and sit cross legged on the floor opposite him. He asks me why I am here; what do I know about Shamanism; what am I hoping will happen during the program?

I tell him as honestly as I can. I'm here because my friend mentioned "Shamanism" in passing. I'm here because I did an Internet search on the word and found his website. I'm here because I'm in need of a path to healing.

He knows something different.

I'm here because Spirit sent me.

We talk for a while and I ask all the questions I can think of, and he tells me about his experience, why he is a Shaman and why he leads the *Spirit Paths* group. As it seems we are about to conclude, I ask him if he thinks I am a good fit for this program. He says I am perfect for the program; exactly in the right spot for transformation to occur. Apparently, many people experience the second phase of their lives when they are in their 40's. I hope he is right, because I need a lot of transforming!

❧

At the first *Spirit Paths* class I meet the five other students, plus Ceci who is our other Shaman mentor. As we go around the circle introducing ourselves, I am feeling suddenly inadequate.

What level of crazy do I think I am to be in this group of people who really seem like they have their crap together and have been walking down this path for a lot longer than me? I feel like a complete fake. I mean, I've only been to one Journey Circle in my entire life, and maybe a couple of times to an Indian powwow. When it is my turn, I hardly know what to say; my tongue is tripping all over itself and my face is red hot with embarrassment.

Fake it 'til you make it…

> *"I am Kerri. I just got divorced and I need help getting my life together. I need a new path. I've always been interested in American Indian heritage because I am 1/16 Cherokee from my mother's side. I've always been drawn to this heritage, but always felt like I didn't belong. When my friend mentioned she was deeply healed by a Shaman, I did an internet search and found this program and it looked good. I wasn't raised with religion, and haven't studied spirituality formally, so this is new to me. Gerry let me in…so…I'm here. I'm looking forward to this experience."*

I feel like a *noob* all over again, bumping into doorways and falling off planks, ineptly attempting to escape from zombies and looking ridiculous. Except this time, I'm sitting facing seven extremely attentive no-bullshit people who are fully engaged and witnessing me.

Double-Gulp.

❧

We spend about half an hour discussing this statement:

*If you are not ready for change
in EVERY aspect of your life,
then personal development work
is not for you.*[41]

I feel like I pretty much up-ended my life, so really not too much more to change as far as I can tell. I'm good with this.

Finally, I have to sign an agreement that states I will attend all meetings of this group over the next 6 months, I will honor the privacy of individuals in the group by not divulging anything shared during sessions, and…

*I commit to being radically honest with myself and others within the Spirit Paths Circle.
I commit to walking The Path of the Spiritual Warrior.*[42]

I sign my name on the dotted line. Bring it baby!

જી

As the first month progresses, we dive into *The Four Agreements* by Don Miguel Ruiz. Learning these four agreements, everything my mother ever told me (*"Don't be so sensitive," "Stop caring what everybody else thinks," "It's not all about you"*) made sense like I've been feeling around in the dark for something and someone finally turned on the light.

Be Impeccable with your Word

Don't take anything personally

Don't make assumptions

Do your best

We spend a great deal of time in class talking about these four agreements and what we each think they mean. I decide to make them soak in by reading and re-reading *The Four Agreements* again, and again, and again. Each time I get to the end, I start back at the beginning. This is because when I start trying to practice these four agreements, I am not doing so well with it. I keep messing up and having to start over.

I start wondering if I have some kind of mental deficiency because really, it makes total sense when I read the book and then, well, I just can't do it! I certainly remember finishing college, so I don't know why it is so hard to follow four little agreements. The book is written to the 9th grade level so anyone can understand the darned thing. It's not complicated.

Or is it?

I start realizing that with spiritual and personal development, the entire game is about awareness and practice and patience. I am rewiring my hard wiring. I learn that I have internal scaffolding that is built from my experiences, how I perceived these experiences through my own distorted filters, and then how I formed agreements with myself about how life is. Dismantling this structure while simultaneously building a new one is like a human-sized game of Jenga; at first it feels pretty stable, and I can remove a few blocks here and there fairly easily. But soon, things start getting really shaky as my old foundation erodes. I feel out of balance. I question myself all the time. I have periods of feeling like a complete failure, followed by pride and joy when I 'get it right' and I am in the flow of personal transformation. No matter how I feel, though, one thing is absolutely clear:

There is no turning back

☙

To relieve stress and get some exercise, I play co-ed soccer weekly, and have for years. One night during an especially difficult period in my spiritual development, my soccer team faces a team that is at least a few levels advanced in skill. Because I have been working on awareness, I realize I am frustrated because I have to face a challenge I am not prepared to face. And I also realize it is a feeling I have about my spiritual quest: I feel a lack of preparedness or energy to face the challenge before me. But the choice tonight is clear: play the game the best you can, or walk off the field.

I play.

ဆ

*"Inturbed: The experience like that of fine silt
on the bottom of a still pool of water. The slightest movement of the water
causes the silt to billow up, perhaps ever so slightly yet noticeably.
In a while, as the pool calms again,
the silt resettles into a different place."*
—Gerry Starnes

ဆ

I am discovering something that I've known for a long time, maybe my entire life: *I am never alone.* As I open my mind and heart to accept (and ask for) help, and as I become more attentive during my daily life, I start witnessing how often Spirit/Universe/God/Life is reaching out to me. The synchronicities are multiplying; or perhaps they have always been there and I am only now paying attention well enough to see it.

For class, one of the daily tasks we must do is to look for a morning messenger when we wake up, before starting to engage with our normal workday routines. On this particular morning, I am in a hurry to get the kids to school and as I walk out the door I am nearly whacked in the face by a huge dragonfly.

Good morning messenger! When I look up dragonfly in my animal spirit reference, I find:

You're being entirely too rational about everything and really need to tap in to your deeper emotions… This is a time when the magic and mystery of life is reawakening for you. It's important now to recharge your psychic energy, which you can do so by regularly meditating. More than simply a change, you're going through a major transformation so enjoy the process! [43]

Another day I am feeling particularly overwhelmed by all the transition I am undergoing. At the end of yoga class, my teacher shares this quote and I almost weep in hearing it:

*"When we walk to the edge of all the light we have and take a step into the
darkness of the unknown,
we must believe that one of two things will happen. Either there will be
something solid for us to stand on, or we will be taught to fly."*
-Frank Outlaw

℘

As I notice and acknowledge the synchronicities surrounding me, I feel a deeper and deeper pull to embrace spirituality.

Growing up, I was not raised with church. My mother grew up in Midwest Texas with my grandmother who was extremely zealous in her dedication to church. After seventeen years of a life built around church, my mother had had enough preaching to last a lifetime. When she moved to Dallas, she never looked back, and never went to church again. She still won't.

Being raised without church didn't mean I wasn't exposed to spiritual conversation. I remember many dinners at my house where my parents and their guests debated about religion, past lives, and soul mates, along with arguing political and social philosophy. It was the 70s.

By the time I was in junior high school, however, it started to matter that I didn't belong to a church. I remember one time a boy had asked me out, but when his mother urged him to ask me "What are you?", and I responded "Uh...a girl?" the offer was rescinded; mostly because my mother said to answer 'humanist.'

My whole life I have felt a presence of something greater than myself. When painting outdoors, I discover a profound connection to this greater-*ness*. It manifests itself to me as a certain magical quality in the air, in the way the sun glows warmly on a flower petal, in the way an entire vista can seem to be breathing and pulsing with life, with the same life that is inside of me. I suppose the concentration required to study the vista, to notice every hue and shape, translate it through my mind, and send that knowledge down to my fingers and onto the paper...this level of concentration is what opens my awareness to the *LIFE* that surrounds me. I feel that this *LIFE* is God.

Throughout my life, painting becomes my way to connect with that power bigger than me, to feel peace and love inside myself. It becomes my way of honoring life, my meditation, my space to work out whatever is frustrating me in my everyday existence. It becomes my method for quieting my mind. I don't ask for anything, except to be connected, to capture how it feels to experience life in the artwork I create.

℞

After my affair, when I am in the throes of despair, simply connecting with the experience of life by being outdoors is not enough for my aching soul. I am so deep in darkness, I cannot see the sunlight. It is during this time that I pray for the first time. Beg is more like it. Much like Elizabeth Gilbert describes in *Eat, Pray, Love*, I am down on the floor of my bathroom sobbing, desperate, and wishing my life could be over.

Please God, Please Help Me

All of a sudden, my tears lift and I feel peaceful acceptance. Like God reached into my heart and turned off the tear spigot. From that moment on, whenever I am in a similar desperation, I simply pray and am always answered with that same relief, that same peace.

During the course of my struggle, I realize that the Valley of the Shadows of Death is absolutely real: it is in our minds. I also know that equally real is the brightest light in the Universe—God.

℞

Although I have complete faith that God is real, this does not mean I am comfortable about going to church. So much of the context of my upbringing has discouraged church-going, has torn down faith with skepticism, has accused church of merely being a business designed to prey upon the weak for their money.

So when I walk through the doors at Unity Church and take a seat, I am taking my own leap of faith (although I am alert for any sign of hypocrisy). As a first-timer at Unity, I am not prepared for the custom whereby I must stand and be identified as a newcomer. I feel completely exposed and uncertain and *unworthy*, that when the minister says "You came in under that Arch as a child of God, already perfect," I cannot help that tears are streaming down my face.

☙

In *Spirit Paths*, I am learning to trust my growing awareness of my physical and energetic experience; I am learning to pay attention to my intuition. I am also learning to refrain from assigning meaning to my experiences, and take a little more time gathering wisdom. Just because something feels different than anything I have ever felt before, it does not mean it is bad, or it is good: It just is.

I am learning to create a tiny sliver of space for interpreting my experience before my mind assigns its automated, learned response. Through this itty bitty window, I am forging myself into the person I want to be: the person I already *am* without all the masks I've been wearing my whole life to make people like me. I am learning to appreciate my imperfection because I am my shadows and my light; I am my glories and my defeats. I am learning to pay attention to that tiny voice when she tells me:

"Follow over here…this is the better way…"

☙

I have started dating a new man, Robb, who lives in North Carolina. We talk endlessly on the phone at night, so much so that I am struggling to get enough sleep so I can wake up in the morning. I enjoy hearing his deep rumbling voice every night, and delight when he calls me for our evening chat. He has been along for the start of my spiritual journey, and tells me that it invigorates him because his own spirituality—rooted in the Baptist faith—has been lackluster.

About a month after we have been talking, we make plans for me to come visit him in North Carolina. When I arrive at the airport, he picks me up in his beater car, even though he has a convertible. He opens my door for me and closes it behind me because the inside door handle does not work. It's a vastly different experience for me than Z who makes a great salary and drives a new Mustang. But I have agreed with myself that I do not care about material wealth, that it is what is inside the person that counts. So I am overlooking the fact that Robb's car won't start and we are in the passenger pickup area at the airport and soon, the police will be asking us what is wrong. In fact, a security officer approaches the vehicle and Robb tells him that the car won't start. This officer has a kind smile and he says, "Try again… I am a good luck charm." The car starts! We all laugh and we are off on our journey.

What I notice about Robb is that he is a self-reliant southern gentleman. He treats me with impeccable kindness at every moment. He caresses my hand, opens the door for me, excuses himself for any perceived impoliteness. He is quite simply a very good person.

He accepts me just the way I am. And even though he is only a few inches taller than me (and extremely fit), he encourages me to lean on him when we are back at his house watching a movie. "You're small. I'm much bigger," he says, and I am so grateful for his kindness. He makes me feel like a desirable woman, like I deserve to be treated well by a man.

Robb shares something with me: he is half Cherokee. His mother is full-blooded Cherokee, but does not practice the old ways. I feel like this common ancestry binds us together in some very special way. When we are asleep later that night, I wake in the middle of the night to absolute darkness and although I cannot see anything, I feel a large presence hovering over the bed. In my dream mind, I feel like I am absolutely awake, and I have an inner *knowing* that this is Robb's soul. It is deep, and ancient, and wise, and I lift my hands to feel it in the darkness. I am so amazed by this experience; and I feel closer to Robb than ever.

I feel this experience must mean something.

ↂ

With my growing awareness, I am discovering not only that I can have experiences that are not typical for the average person in our society, but that I have a very active disaster mind.

When Robb does not respond to my text or phone message for two days because he is on a modeling shoot in Ontario, I go deep into worst case scenarios complete with tears and full-on rejection that leads to nasty-grams fired off to his phone.

My disaster mind is hard at work:

> *He doesn't like me anymore.*
> *I'm not good enough for him.*
> *He is with another woman.*
> *She's a model…and prettier and thinner than me.*
> *He got into a car accident and is dying in an emergency room.*
> *If he doesn't like me, then fine. Fuck him.*
> *I should just end it right now.*
> *It's not working out anyway.*

Of course, I mentally counter all of these fearful beliefs when they arise, but they are overwhelming.

I decide to try something new. I get a journal and on each page, I draw a line down the middle. On the outer side of the page I write all the crazy ramblings of my disaster mind. On the inner side of the page, I write rational thoughts of what could be happening.

> *I don't know why he is unavailable today.*
> *My day was filled with excitement and I am*
> *just disappointed I can't share it with him.*
> *I have a good life. Everything is fine.*
> *I am.*

To actively disengage disaster mind, I tear out the outer side of the page and ritualistically burn it while I intention verbally that I am releasing these negative thoughts because they no longer serve me. When I see these disaster thoughts going up in flame, I feel like I am banishing them to the far reaches of the Universe. Now the only story that remains is the one my rational self wrote on the inside of the page.

I am rewriting my story.
I am rewiring my mind.
I am rebuilding the Jenga structure of my Self.

☙

In addition to all the reading for my Spirit Paths class, I am reading every self-help, personal development, and spiritual guidance book that is recommended to me. I spend hours reading and soaking up all this wisdom. I figure maybe all this wisdom will fertilize the soil of my mind so that as I am rebuilding my Jenga structure, I will have more solid ground on which to support my new spiritual home.

After reading *A Return to Love* by Marianne Williamson, I begin wearing a silver acorn necklace, and inside of it I place the citrine stone that Ceci has given me. This little acorn reminds me that every thought and word is a seed in my spiritual garden.

I want to grow lushness in my spiritual garden. I remind myself to pay attention:

Thoughts are seeds we germinate to grow our spiritual garden. Cultivate acceptance, peace, joy and love and your garden will thrive in the sunshine, and nourish itself in the wisdom gained from rain.

Wearing the citrine stone around my neck, so close to my heart, cleanses all my negative energy and transforms it into clarity and peace.

☙

Suggestions

Stop Focusing on Your Story! Our thoughts create our reality. By focusing our thoughts on reliving the past, or by telling the same version of our history again and again, we cement the story as the one and only REALITY which makes it very hard to change the story into a better one. Develop awareness of the story you tell yourself. Look for ways to create a NEW story for yourself by changing your perspective of the facts.

Listen! Pay attention to your disaster mind. What is it telling you in the background of your daily life? The only way to feel better is to rewrite that disaster story into a love story, or action-adventure, or comedy. Whatever YOU prefer! Make that mind work for YOU! Be sure to write it down so you can witness what your mind is telling you.

Try Everything with Total Abandon! If it has healed someone else, it might work for you. So try it. Sure: You might feel strange listening to wisdom from a manufactured game. But if it works...if it gives _you_ insight...do you care _HOW_ it works?? Just try everything.

Notice Your Teachers! The synchronicities of the people and situations in our lives are not haphazard... they are intentional. So pay attention! If you are working on being alone for the first time, and you suddenly have a connection with someone who has been alone for the last 10 years..._this is not an accident_. Go with it! Take the invitation and open your eyes and ears to learn from this new teacher.

Ask for Help! (and take it) I have heard it said that God /Angels /Spirits can't give you help until you ask for it. **So ask.** When you are asking from your heart for help because you truly, deeply need guidance, _help is delivered_. Be mindful that you will receive what you _need_ : which may not be what you _want_.

Follow Your Intuition! That little voice inside your head has been drowned out by all the noise and clutter of your daily life. When you make space and connect with the world around you, when you slow down, you start hearing this little voice more and more. Listen to it! It is your higher self, and *that* you KNOWS A LOT!

Quotes

"Spirituality is recognizing and celebrating that we are all inextricably connected to each other by a power greater than all of us, and that our connection to that power and to one another is grounded in love and compassion. Practicing spirituality brings a sense of perspective, meaning and purpose to our lives." — Brené Brown[44]

"A wise farmer will tell you that planting a seed takes a few seconds. The real value is in the preparation of the soil. Fertile fields produce lush crops. That abundant beautiful life you want? That's one very lush crop."
— Janet Conner[45]

"I describe these internal foundations as a type of scaffolding that we create throughout our lives. This scaffolding is based on lies we are told about ourselves, distortions of what's true, false beliefs we take on, stories we create to explain things, and emotions we attach to our experiences. This scaffolding starts to weaken and crumble as we continue to shine our light of awareness and truth on it. As we peel away the layers of illusion, false beliefs, stories, and emotional distortions we've accumulated, space is created for a new foundation, and a structure to be built in its place, one that is based on our present truth."
— Cecilia Zuniga[46]

"Development of a personal mantra, and the act of ritualization is powerful. Work it, craft it, repeat it, and fashion it into another tool in your skill set."
— Chrispy Bhagat Singh47

"What we achieve inwardly will change outer reality."
—Plutarch

Journaling

I honestly cannot believe that I never journaled before this part of my life. It's such a useful tool. Using it to bring awareness to your disaster mind is extremely powerful because once you see what you are really thinking, you will see that _your mind is lying to you_. Consider this: if a friend said those things to you about themself, how would you respond?

Burning disaster mind thoughts is a potent practice because fire is transformation. Send your intention to stop believing a thought into the flames, and then write a new story to replace the old, outdated one. You _are_ what you _believe_!

As recommended by Janet Connor in her book The Lotus and the Lily, journaling to engage your soul is very powerful work. In this type of journaling, you pose questions to your higher self, to Spirit, to God, to the Universe, in your journal, and then just write as quickly as you can whatever comes into your awareness without judging it. Just write it! Sometimes, the answers you seek come in dreams, or in synchronicities in waking life. When you practice this type of writing, I _promise_ you will be astounded at the insights you receive.

Healing the Original Wound

I decide to use one of the one-on-one sessions included with my *Spirit Paths* program to do a healing session with my Shaman mentor, Gerry. We meet at his office off South 1st Street, settle cross-legged on the floor, and take a few deep breaths. As usual, Gerry pulsates with energy like the fumes emanating from a fire. He picks up his drum and spends a while drumming, letting the rhythm of the drum loosen our minds into biorhythm and heart space. He then asks me what I want to accomplish with this session, why I am here.

I tell him I am tired of carrying this burden of sadness. That I need help healing this wounding, this borderline personality disorder that is making it so I cannot maintain trust in a love relationship. This is a deep wound that I now understand has permeated the entire fabric of my relationship with men, and the experience of my life.

Gerry explains that his wisdom comes from Spirit. It is not until he is in trance that he will be in a sacred dance with Spirit whereby he will perform whatever healing is necessary. He briefly describes some things that might happen during our session, but repeats that he does not know what will actually happen until he can be advised by Spirit.

I lay on the floor and try to relax as Gerry smudges the room with burning white sage and begins to drum, getting into the Spirit trance. After several minutes, my mind begins to question this experience: "I don't feel anything", "This isn't working". I remind myself to trust in Spirit and the process and let go of expectation.

A few moments later I feel this layer of energy, of presence, hovering above me, and instantly Gerry stops drumming. I know this is no coincidence: Spirit has arrived.

Gerry is preparing something, and I lay still and relaxed, waiting for the healing process to begin. Soon he is pulling something from my breast bone. Literally I can feel something being tugged free of me, from the area right in the middle of my chest. This is the area that I have often felt a sort of dark smudge, an emptiness, a yearning, whenever I am in emotional pain over a love relationship. He is pulling this *something* out of me and flicking it into the smoldering ashes of the white sage. And how I know he is doing this I do not know, because my eyes are closed. But I just know.

Next, he is pulling gently down my forearms, down my fingers, and removing this *something* from my arms, and flicking it into the smoldering ashes.

Once this finishes, he is rustling around for something, which he then places inside my left hand. It feels like a stick. He breathes something into my hand into the stick, and then places that hand over my heart, and puts my right hand over it. As soon as he does this, I burst into tears. I don't know why. I just do.

When he finishes, he rises and says "Rest. I will be back with some water." I lay there, crying, not knowing what just happened, but feeling immensely relieved.

Gerry returns and when we are seated facing one another again he tells me what has happened. It seems that Spirit has shown him a series of still pictures of the trauma I experienced as a toddler with my father in the bathtub. And here is the story….

I am in the tub with my Daddy. I love my Daddy. And he and I are having a wonderful bath together. In fact, I am making Daddy very happy because I am making it grow. Daddy is showing me how to make it grow with my hands. And I love my Daddy and he loves me. Everything is right in the world.

Then my Mommy comes into the bathroom and she sees what is happening. Suddenly there is overwhelming SHAME. I love my Mommy, so I take her shame into myself and I store it right in the center of my being. I cover my arms with shame gloves because they are what did the bad thing that made Mommy so upset.

Now it all makes sense.

I was biting my arms because they did the bad thing that made Mommy so upset. I wanted to bite them off and make Mommy happy again.

This story is so much more than abandonment. I was an active participant in my Daddy going away. I was the cause, and I held the shame.

So every time a man has not responded to me, every time he has disappeared, every time he has rejected me, I have felt that shame again, and again, and again.

When my mother came into the room and I took her shame, I also lost a piece of my soul. My innocence fled right out of my little toddler body. During Shamanic soul retrieval, Gerry accessed that soul part and put it into a crystal, the 'stick', and put it into my hand and over my heart. Whether that was actually my soul part, or Gerry's intention of my soul part, I felt it energetically and it made me burst into tears at having it returned to me.

In the weeks and months following this session, I notice that I do not feel the black hole inside my chest any longer. It is gone. My being feels much more grounded and full than ever before in my life.

It's like Spirit was able to work through Gerry to take out of me what all those hours and years of therapy never could quite remove. I realize there is more to life than I understand; that it is possible there are deep wounds that cannot be healed by simply talking about them.

જી

It ended so quietly...not with a bang, but a whisper.
I finally understand softness, and being the river.
The puzzle pieces all fell together and made perfect simple sense. The dark smudge at the core of my being disappeared, and there is finally acceptance, forgiveness, and peace inside my heart.

જી

The next time I see my mother, she wants to know what happened during my appointment with Gerry. I feel unsure about telling her because I sense the guilty burden she carries is so great. But I succumb to her desire and I tell her "I know why I was biting my arms Mom. I was helping Daddy making it grow." She is instantly reaching for me, to cover this up, this awful shameful TRUTH. I pull away, but with kindness in my eyes and love in my heart. This shame does not belong to me.

∞

Try clutching wet sand and you can hold onto it forever. Try clutching dry sand and it slips between your fingers. I'm going to let this sand dry out, open my fingers, and let it slip through and disappear.

Suggestions

Relinquish Control! You do not need to know WHY something works to know that it works. If you experience healing, no matter how it happened, you are healed. So let go of trying to reconcile the experience with your mind and knowledge of the world, and let it be. I believe this is one way at looking at the story of the Garden of Eden. In many ways, our quest for knowledge to explain our experience of life is what keeps us from actually _living_ and deeply connecting with what our higher self knows to be true: we are still in the Garden...we never left it.

Trust Your Intuition! More than ever, when you are experiencing things you have never experienced before, you must trust your own intuition. Build your own healing experience and rituals by trusting yourself and the healers in whom you decide to put your faith. When doubt comes knocking, dismiss it because it is fear: give into _your_ experience.

Heal the Original Wound! The first time we were wounded is what keeps us stuck in our patterns. Heal that, and you can move on.

Quotes

"As you align yourself, your attention, your intention, and your energy with this path, things begin to move and shift. You arrive at new levels of awareness, and dormant parts of yourself begin to stir and awaken. It's like taking a flashlight to the dark corners of a room you've lived in for years, but never fully explored. Suddenly, the light shines on things you had no idea were there, and you see them for the first time, and everything you thought you knew about that room and your life in it changes." — Cecilia Zuniga[48]

"Don't be hard like a rock, be soft like water. Ultimately the soft wins over the hard. Be like water, soft, flowing, at ease. The hardness inside will eventually be reduced to sand, and the rock will completely disappear."
— Laozi

"It is better to conquer yourself than to win a thousand battles. Then the victory is yours. It cannot be taken from you, not by angels or by demons, heaven or hell."
—Buddha

"In my healing practice, I find that only when we discover our original wound can true understanding follow. In the West we suffer from what I call 'premature evaluation' —the more rapidly we name something, tag it, categorize it, and try to understand it, the more quickly we shortchange the deep transformation taking place." — Alberto Villoldo, Ph.D.[49]

"Once the soul part is lost, there is an energetic pattern set that can be seen to recur in the person's life. Often the client has a thought or behavior pattern that keeps returning, like being unable to enter a dark place or being unable to maintain intimate relationships. These patterns generally are based on unreasonable fears, the source of which eludes the client. So the effects of the original soul loss repeat over and over in a person's life." —Gerry Starnes, M.Ed.[50]

"I'm trying to free your mind, Neo. But I can only show you the door. You're the one that has to walk through it." —Morpheus[51]

Shamanism

I thought I would take a brief moment to talk about contemporary Shamanism since it is such a large part of my healing, and my story.

In my opinion, humans living in the modern world have become very disconnected from our natural context, from the world we live in, from the Earth. Technology, such as electricity and artificial light, has made it so that we can exist without reliance on nature, without understanding the natural rhythms and cycles of life. As we proceed into cyberspace, we move further from the natural world into a world for our minds. We journey away from our hearts, from our intuition, from God/Spirit/Universal Energy, and from the Earth.

Similar to the need Yoga fills, Shamanism connects us back to the Earth, to the energy of animals and plants, to the natural rhythms of life, and to our intuition and capacity for dreaming from heart center. Shamanism connects us back with Spirit, our ephemeral guides, our higher knowing, and the Universe. It is as ancient and healing as sitting by the campfire, watching the flame and telling stories.

Straddling Worlds

Gerry says I need to keep my crystal with me at all times because I need to coax my lost soul part back into my being; I need to demonstrate that it's safe inside me for the innocent little girl to reunite with me. That part of me has been missing for most of my life; she doesn't know me at all. I tape a picture of myself at two on my bathroom mirror. I want to welcome that part of myself, my innocence, to return and reside within me. Seeing this little girl as a separate entity, a separate part of me, I realize that if I saw her skipping down the sidewalk I'd want to be her mother in an instant! I'd scoop her up and steal her. It helps me realize that if I love that little girl, I love myself too.

One night I am feeling emotional about this lovely little girl with red curly locks, and in the shower I visualize holding her tight against my chest. I tell her it is safe now, she doesn't need to be afraid. I'm all grown up and I can take care of her. I can be her mommy. I'm a good mommy.

ભ

I'm starting to notice that, in fact, I am a good mom. I have managed over the last several years to maintain connection with my sons despite my mental absence. I have managed to give my boys enough love and attention every day that they want to be with me on the days it is my 'turn' to be parent. When they are with me, I take extra care to be present to them, to stay in the moment with my boys.

However, parenting as a single mom who is dating is not without its challenges. At some point when I am dating Robb, even though we only talk late at night after the boys are in bed, my son Tanner (then 9) spits bitterly at bedtime one night "I guess you want me to go to sleep so you can talk to Robb."

Rather than letting my inner judge take this accusation and wound me with it, I use my new awareness to create a sliver of space for consideration. I tell Tanner, "No. It's simply time for you to sleep so you can awake fresh in the morning. I love you. Now, good night," and with a hug and kiss I leave his room.

Clearly, my son is feeling second shrift in the Mommy attention department. So the next night, I announce that we have a new bedtime ritual. Tanner will get dressed for bed half an hour early and climb under the sheets so I can read him a book for thirty minutes.

Tanner and Mommy time. Just the two of us. Undivided attention from Mommy.

Tanner loves this idea, and I do not hear any more hateful statements from him about Robb. In fact, he asks me a couple of weeks later if things are going well with Robb, if he will ever meet him. I tell him I don't know yet. Not enough time has passed. Silently, I am happy because I have successfully straddled the line between mommy and woman.

ભ

Although I am divorced, I am not free of my ex-husband. Co-parenting requires a lot of collaboration, especially because my older son Garrett is struggling in school. Going back and forth between our homes every other night is wearing thin on the children. The rules at my house are few: get your homework done to the best of your ability, study until you are ready to do well on tests, treat each other with respect. Beyond this, my house offers the boys a great deal of freedom as to how they choose to spend their free time. Most times, we are each in our own rooms, pursuing our own interests quietly. Life at their dad's house is the opposite: there is always something that needs to be done, and there is a structure to every moment of every day. There are a lot of rules to be followed, and the children often see his punishments as arbitrary and unfair.

Since Tom and I have such different styles, it has always been a challenge co-parenting. When we lived together, I often found myself between him and the children on this issue or that. We have never agreed on a common strategy.

Now that we live in separate houses, I have more freedom to parent as I see fit in my own domicile. However, Tom continually tries to interject his will into my sphere of influence and sometimes I find this frustrating. I am especially frustrated when Tom expects me to enforce punishment on the kids, and I have not been part of the discussion about the punishment.

Where is the rightful home of anger when ownership of your life and choices belongs squarely on your own shoulders? I chose to spend 20 years with a person who worked to control me and undermine my self-esteem. And I allowed it to happen. So now that I choose *not* to allow that control over my life and choices, do I have a right to feel angry when this person continues the same behavior, this time regarding our children?

Can I be angry that he is being his authentic self? Can I allow my growing awareness of the pattern of interaction with him, and how it makes me feel that my judgment and experience are not valued by him, to anger me? Does he need to value my judgment and experience? Is his valuation necessary for my self-evaluation?

છ

When the last day of school arrives, I am glad to be done with the first school year as a divorced family, and I surprise my boys with a trip to the beach down at Port Aransas, on the coast of Texas. Just the three of us. The first night we make the drive down to Corpus Christie, and when we check into the hotel we put on our bathing suits and head to the pool.

I jump in head first, getting my hair all wet, and a huge grin spreads across Tanner's face as he exclaims "Water Mommy is baaaaack!" Apparently it's been years since I have gotten my hair wet in the pool. I'm glad I'm fun again. I frolic in the water with my boys and have a wonderful time playing and laughing and giggling with them.

Afterwards we get dressed and wander down the street for dinner. I find an Italian restaurant on Yelp that has great reviews, so we walk over there from the hotel. When we enter the restaurant, I see the white table cloths and have a moment of panic. But then, I breathe, and trust my sons can handle this new experience. We sit down and I explain about putting the napkin in their laps, and speaking softly, and then we look over the menu. Each boy orders a dish, and when it arrives, they are tentative at first, and then they enjoy this new expression of pasta and ravioli like they have never before eaten a meal. I teach Tanner to wind the pasta on his fork using his spoon (rather than sucking it up like he usually does at home), and he enjoys eating like a big boy.

When they finish, they each are surprised to have enjoyed something new. My older son Garrett (then 12) says "Mommy, I want to come eat here all the time!" I am vastly rewarded by this because Garrett is a notoriously picky eater; he has existed like one of those air plants that somehow survives with mere mist.

When we arrive at the beach hotel in Port Aransas the next day I am enjoying watching the boys playing in the sand, building castles and forts and lagoons. Occasionally, I text Robb, and I don't hear a response, but I work hard to stay in the moment.

Later in the afternoon my friend Lindsay from *Spirit Paths* joins us on the beach and we enjoy wading in the breaking waves with the boys, laughing for hours as the waves crash into us, knocking us over in the surf.

My mind keeps wandering to Robb, wondering why he is not responding to me, but I continually refocus my thoughts on the moment. I'm with my boys at the beach, my place is right here right now.

I see so many pelicans flying overhead, and it seems they pause right over me, or in front of me; it seems they are always hovering there. When I get back to my phone I look up pelicans in my animal spirit reference, and I discover some very useful advice from Spirit.

The pelican teaches that no matter how difficult life becomes, no matter how much you plunge—you can pop to the surface. The pelican holds the knowledge of how to rise above life's trials.

Pelicans, in spite of their lightness, sometimes have a difficult time taking off from the water. Still they do manage, and again we can see the correspondence to freeing oneself from that which would weigh you down. The water is a symbol of emotions, and emotions often weigh us down. The pelican teaches us how not to be overcome by them.[52]

As the afternoon wears on, and I do not have any messages from Robb, I become more anxious. Lindsay and I take the boys for a late lunch. I decide to eat crab legs: Lindsay and I laugh that eating crab is an excellent way to stay in the moment because to eat, you have to focus on getting the crab meat out of all those legs!

For most of the day, I am able to stay focused on being in the moment with my boys and my friend. I am able to quiet my disaster mind. But by the evening, when all the activity dies down, I realize I have only postponed the inevitable: disaster mind strikes and before long I am outside the room while the boys sleep, sending Robb a video telling him I know he is cheating on me and I have to break it off because I can't trust him. I turn off my phone and go to sleep, quietly crying so as not to wake my sons.

When I wake in the middle of the night I see Robb has texted me. He has tried to call me but my phone is off, and he leaves me a message to the effect that he is accepting the end to our relationship. I am so upset with myself for once again allowing my disaster mind, my BPD, my *crazy*, to ruin my life.

I text him back that I am sorry. I've told him how I struggle with my mind before; he understands, but then again, he really does not understand. How can he? He doesn't struggle the way I do with my savage thoughts.

The next morning Robb texts me back, then calls, and we are reunited. He wants to understand what happens inside my mind. I simply want to stop the madness. Why can't I just be happy in the moment with my sons on the beach? Why do I have to create a drama out of nothing?

ଔ

When I see Chrispy the next time, I am very much struggling with this reoccurrence of disaster mind. Why does this keep happening to me when I no longer want to behave this way? When I am aware that what is going on in my mind is nonsense, why can't I stop mid-tracks? Why can't I let go and trust? Why do I keep cycling back and repeating the same behaviors?

Chrispy explains to me that Spirit never stops sending us the situations: we will encounter our personal nemesis again, and again, and again. What changes is not whether we experience our challenge, because we will experience it again and again; what changes is our relationship with it, our response to it, when it occurs.

He describes life as a great spiral, circling ever higher and outwards so that when we circle back around to our personal challenge, we can look downwards and inwards and see all the times we crossed this challenge before along our journey. That ability to witness and have awareness offers the opportunity for a different response each time we encounter our nemesis. Eventually, perhaps we even get to a space of clarity where we can laugh when the challenge presents itself yet again.

I am very doubtful I will ever laugh at this.

"Continue the work," he says. "With greater awareness comes the possibility for different responses, and new outcomes."

⚘

In the meantime, even though it is summer, there are clashes of the Titans over summertime plans between my ex-husband, my parents, and myself. It seems the struggles of co-parenting (three-way!) never end.

After reflection one afternoon, I visualize parenting as a tightrope that I am delicately walking between adopting strategies from my parents that 'worked' for me growing up and navigating new horizons for ideas to fill the gaps in parenting that didn't 'work' for me as a child. I am trying hard to respect my family history while infusing its 'story' with new life from other influences that I have been experiencing lately in my life. All of this while collaborating with people (Tom and my parents) who are passionately and deeply invested in the subject of all this work—my sons.

My sons will not know for another 20 years how we have labored over their daily transformations.

∝

My struggles with men are not over, it seems. I continue to have trouble with my disaster mind whenever I don't hear from my boyfriend Robb. As I am in the middle of creating drama from nothing one Saturday night, I am on the floor rolling around because I'm attempting to do anything I can NOT to send any nasty grams to this poor man, and see under my bed a folded piece of paper that I know fell out of a journal I recently rediscovered from when I was 22. Reading it, I am surprised (and not) to read my own writing say that my boyfriend from college said I created my own stress because I liked having it in my life. I wrote that I disagreed.

Well..honey...
you sho' 'nough did
and always have!

Ha! I burst out in laughter at myself then and now. I guess it is possible to laugh at my nemesis, at my disaster mind.

Welcome to enlightenment.

∝

One Sunday in early summer, the sermon at my church is "Who is your hero?" I think of my mother. She changed her entire life, and faced extremely frightening situations at the risk of personal injury or even death, to protect her child. Many women do not take the risks she did. They turn their backs and pretend they do not see what is right in front of them. She did not. At a time when courts in Dallas insisted on photographic evidence of abuse, my mother dared to take me and run. She protected me at the risk of arrest. She lived in fear of my natural father hunting me down, hiding with the drapes drawn for the better half of my childhood.

I visit my mother after church and tell her that she is my hero. When I tell her this, I feel a shift occur inside of her. She cries and we hold each other. It feels good to send this healing her way, to heal the shame she has felt all these years.

∽

I am about to become a full-time employee for my biggest client, so I decide to take a last hurrah. I plan a two-week trip to the Smoky Mountains to camp and visit Cherokee Nation. I have always wanted to know more about this aspect of my heritage, and I am excited to go camping again to the woods. It has been years since I have been camping. Plus, it is very handy that when I get to the other side of the Smoky Mountains, I will be able to meet Robb in Asheville, North Carolina and have a visit. We haven't seen each other for a couple of months, and I am missing him.

My friends and family are concerned about me camping alone in the woods; they think something bad will happen to me in the woods that wouldn't have happened any of the times I have traveled to distant places for art shows.

I am not worried; I am excited. This is the first vacation I have ever taken by myself.

It takes a couple of days to drive from Texas to the Smoky Mountains. The road is long, but it is a chance to listen to all of my favorite music and sing and sing and sing. I am excited about the entire journey, and especially about the first stop to visit with Robb.

When I arrive in Asheville, I am struck by what a quaint town it is with its unique eateries and specialty mom & pop stores. I park and walk until I find a restaurant with sidewalk dining and get myself a café au lait which comes in a huge cup that could be from the Mad Hatter's Tea Party. I am enjoying people-watching and eating my French toast with apple slices dripping in syrup. I am comfortable and happy in my solitude amongst other people out and about on this lovely Friday morning.

I peruse the shops, drifting in and out, enjoying the freedom of wandering without any specific place to be. I cannot remember the last time I ventured around aimlessly like this, and I am relishing the moment.

I make an appointment at a local salon for a pedicure and settle into the luxury of pampering in a dimly lit spa off the main street.

My text beeps: Robb is on the way!

As he arrives to town there is a brief rain shower which I am enjoying, but he is not. I have returned to the outdoor eatery to seek shelter from its awning while I wait for the rain to stop so he can join me in this café.

When Robb joins me it is not as I expected; he is irritable which interrupts the harmonious warm glow I have had all afternoon. I figure perhaps it is just the three hour drive to Asheville that has him out of sorts. And it seems that is the case because after a visit to the hotel, we return downtown much happier, and just in time for the community drum circle.

"Oh wow!" I exclaim, and I decide I want to participate. So I trot back to the car and grab my drum which I have brought with me on this journey, and as I walk back through town with my shamanic journey drum I feel just fine publicly owning this part of my identity.

I settle into the crowd of drummers and start contributing my own rhythm to the community of sound and it feels wonderful. Robb is smiling and moving his head to the beat from the 'audience' area around the drummers, enjoying this experience as much as I am from the 'drummer' side, feeling the drums move through our bodies, joining everyone in this circle to one large shared human experience.

As the lead drummers pack up to continue their evenings on their individual paths, I decide it is time to move on as well. I have discovered that there is a female singer-songwriter performing at the local theatre, and Robb agrees to come along. We settle into seats in this intimate setting, and the performance begins. Soon it is dawning on me that this singer is lesbian, and that many of the women in the audience are as well. I am comfortable in this environment because I studied at Smith which is an all-women's Ivy League college; but as a devout Baptist, I am not so sure about Robb's viewpoints.

In fact, during the break, Robb discloses that he has figured out that this singer is lesbian. But he is open to continuing to listen. He is interested in her story, and he is enjoying hearing her accompanist sing because he says her voice resonates as if God is singing through her.

At one point, the singer touches Robb's heart with her words and tears are streaming down his face. I am attracted to this man who can feel such depth that it moves him to cry, and that he does so in public without shame. The other women notice as well, and are patting his back and welcoming him into their circle after the performance. He has won their hearts too.

Following the performance, Robb confirms his suspicions about the accompanist when he asks her if she is a believer. In fact, she is. She has been born again after having lost faith. Now, she says, her singing is renewed with strength and glory and an effortless delivery. I am intrigued by everything being shared between Robb and this accompanist because I feel like there is truth here, even though my upbringing would lead me to an initial critical reaction.

Afterwards, Robb is so energized by his talk with this woman that he is sharing ideas and experiences of his own over the last several months and it is a different man in front of me. He is glowing. And I am in love with this man, with his faith and positive energy.

We get into a debate about God, and for the first time in my life, I feel I have something to say about the subject. Robb has immense faith in the Bible, and can recount numerous verses and details about Jesus and how we are meant to live in the world. I do not have this knowledge; I have only my experience of a higher power. And I speak from it. I tell Robb that I believe it is far simpler what God wants of us. God wants us to love, to be happy, to live and enjoy life, to grow and be the best we can be. The energy that is everywhere in everything is God. And that Universal energy does not care what nationality you are, or your ethnicity, or how you conceive of it with your religious beliefs. Many faces, many windows into the same truth. I feel so passionate about expressing my point of view, and he listens. His upbringing teaches him differently, but he is able to listen and accept my truth as my own. What is more: I am able to express my beliefs with confidence.

The next day we go to see the Botanical Gardens which are absolutely lovely. While we are there, I walk out onto the rocks on the stream and put my feet into the gurgling waters as I sit on a large boulder. I coax Robb out into the stream, and he comes reluctantly. He takes off one sandal and puts his toe into the river. I smile. I don't truly understand this man that comes from such a different version of the world than the one where I have been raised. But it seems that despite our differences, we are getting along well and having a very nice time together. Until we reach the car after our walk.

It is now that Robb starts asking me how I can feel love for him, because I have told him that I do. He asks me what is it about him that I love? I tell him the many things about being with him that I enjoy, that I enjoy the way his energy feels with mine, that I enjoy talking with him and sharing life experiences and thoughts.

And then he turns my heart inside out.

I should feel the same way about you.
You're everything I've wanted for myself.
So I just don't understand why I don't love you.

 C8

He is holding me and with one hand lifting my chin, he is trying to force me to look him in the eyes; all I want to do is run away. He is clearly just as troubled by his feelings as I am hearing them. I know he is not trying to hurt me, but the pain of this is more than I can bear. He is telling me how awful he feels to see me hurt. He doesn't want to hurt me this way. I tell him to go. After he takes his bag and leaves, I go into my hotel room and lay in the darkened room.

After crying for several hours, it dawns on me that I am repeating my pattern. Once again, I think a relationship is going in one direction, based on my feelings, and then it turns out it is heading in the exact opposite direction because my feelings aren't shared by the other half of the equation—the *man*.

I come to a realization. All I have is myself. And I'm in the middle of a beautiful mountain town at the foothills of the Smoky Mountains. The sun is shining outside of my darkened room, and I am on vacation, and I am loved by someone on this planet still: *me*. I come to the awareness that a year ago, I would have chosen to respond very differently to this circumstance. A year ago, I could have chosen to hurt myself in my despair and shame and self-loathing. But today: I am aware that I have a choice in how I respond to this unexpected disclosure. I am also aware that harming myself is no longer an option.

I pick up my journal, and turn pain into poetry.

> *A tiny river pools and plummets,*
> *meandering from the crease of salty lashes,*
> *sliding down freckled hillock,*
> *evaporating as it meets air,*
> *until it is only a memory*
> *of unrequited love.*

After a great deal of reflection after Robb departs, I come to a decision: it is time to let go of what I *think* I want, and embrace what the current moment has to offer me.

> *Sometimes we cling to something*
> *out of fear of what we will be without it,*
> *but it is precisely release of outmoded attachments that is a prerequisite for*
> *growth and transformation to a more authentic and fulfilling existence.*
> *Tonight I have opened my hand*
> *and released the little bird*
> *that was clutched in my grasp.*
> *Fly and be free...*

My heart has been broken again. Yet I am still standing. My roots have sunk deeper into the black soil of the Earth, weaving and winding their way past boulders and debris. I stand tall as I head into the Smoky Mountains, alone.

08

A tiny lobster claws at my bum as I sit on a rock in the stream at the campground where I am staying. When I look down at it, it reaches its little claws up to me through the top of the water and waves them at me as if to be picked up. When I get back to my tent, I look up lobster (since this little guy is a craw daddy).

> *You're in the midst of a powerful process*
> *of transformation in which you'll find yourself*
> *trying out different expressions of who you are throughout each phase. One*
> *of your big lessons*
> *right now is patience, particularly in learning to*
> *wait for whatever you need to come to you*
> *rather than pursuing it.*[53]

In this moment I come to terms with a realization that has been dawning at the back of my mind. I do have love for Robb, even though his life has led a very different course from mine. But I have never stopped wishing for Z. And perhaps this bit of wisdom from the spirit guide *Craw Dad* explains this paradox: how I can feel love for two very different men, how I can be two very different people, in less than a year.

I am transforming. I am trying out different expressions of who I am. I was in a relationship, part of a couple, for my entire adult life—from 22 to 42. It's no wonder I don't really know who I am. I've only just gotten the space to discover all the possibilities and potentialities of *me*.

I realize something really important: I don't have to have it all figured out. It's ok to not know all the answers, or where this is all going. In fact, it would be frustrating and impossible to attempt to control the outcome of this transformation, this becoming.

I am free to follow my heart wherever it leads me.

∞

My visit to Cherokee Nation begins with Oconaluftee Indian Village which is a replica of a replica of a 1750s Cherokee village. Everyone who works at this living museum is a full blooded Cherokee. Somewhere in my distant ancestry, I might even be related to any one of these people.

I enjoy hearing about the customs of the people, how they reared their children, how they conducted tribal business, how they fed and clothed themselves, and mostly, what they believed about spirituality. I feel a distant connection, a vibration back through time, a belonging. And that feels wonderful because it blends with my budding education in Shamanism.

My guide and I talk about how I might use trance in a sweat lodge and ancestral walks back through time to find my lineage, my Cherokee family, since traditional ways of researching ancestry have not worked. My great-great grandmother passed for white during the time following the Trail of Tears; she left the people to pursue her future with a white man, and was excommunicated. I show him a picture of her daughter, my great-grandmother, and the Cherokee heritage is striking in her visage.

I have bent the ear of my guide so long, that he realizes suddenly it is time for the tribal dance. "Come along!" he says… "But…I don't know the dances…" I hesitate. And he laughs. "We need an extra girl. You can follow along…I promise!"

So I chuck my bag and join the fun. And *oh*! It is delightful to dance as if I am one of them, one of the Cherokee dancers performing for the crowd the dances from our shared heritage. It comes naturally, and feels liberating and embracing. Afterwards I have a moment of feeling exposed for being a poser, but then several people who have watched the performance come up to me and compliment me on my dancing. They think I am one of the people who work here. I am delighted. But I guess they do not know that only full blooded Cherokee can work on the reservation.

ભ

I visit the Museum of the Cherokee Indian to dive into more detail about my heritage. And I wonder if maybe there is a historian on staff who can help me with my quest to find my Cherokee roots. I inquire at the front desk. But the response I get is far different than the reception with the people at Oconaluftee Indian Village. The boy working the desk who is in his early 20s looks at the picture of my great-grandmother who is half-blooded Cherokee and says: "You'll never find her. She doesn't exist. She left the people, and the people don't care for her anymore."

I am so profoundly wounded by his words, and a deep dark anger burns inside my soul. This anger is bigger and more fearsome than any feeling I could possess about his words all on my own. It feels like my very blood is fueled with hostility and resentment.

I turn from him and walk into the Museum, determined not to let his hatefulness ruin my opportunity to learn more about my heritage. After winding my way through the exhibit, I come to the powerful realization that my very *blood* is my bond to my heritage, and no one can take that away from me.

As I leave the Museum, I see that boy, and I scorch him with my gaze. I realize I have cursed myself by returning his hatred, and I am disappointed I could not be better than that, for my ancestors.

ભ

I find a spot where three rivers converge into one and I sit on a rock near the middle and play my drum. I play softly at first, and then louder to match the roaring of the water over the boulders. Ancestral spirits gather around to listen. With my eyes closed, I feel them in the trees surrounding the river, all around me.

ભ

When I lay at night peering up through the transparent netting of my tent, the trees of the Smoky Mountains stretch over me to the stars that twinkle in the night sky. Fireflies collide with the tent walls, bursting flashes of light here, then there. It is wondrous to lay there in the stillness, witnessing the beauty of night.

I awake in the morning fresh with remembrance of a very vivid dream, unlike anything I have ever dreamed before. Before I forget it, I write it down.

Old-timey playing cards are being shuffled
to me, but instead of traditional face cards,
mine are embellished with western-style images of
Fox
Wolf
Bear
Raven

Fox

The fox is a totem that has touched almost every society on the planet. It is a totem that speaks of the need to develop or the awakening of camouflage, invisibility, and shapeshifting. It is one of the most uniquely skilled and ingenious animals of nature. It can teach these skills to those whose life it enters....As you develop attunement to the fox and learn its magic, any prize can fall to you. [54]

Wolf

The wolf teaches you to know who you are and to develop strength, confidence and surety in that ...Wolf can teach you how to use ritual to establish order and harmony within your own life. Wolf helps us to understand that true freedom requires discipline. ...The wolf has...the ability to reflect the archetypal forces associated with psychic insight....The wolf has a capacity for making quick and firm emotional attachments... It will guard you as it teaches you—sometimes strongly, sometimes gently—but always with love. When wolf shows up, it is time to breathe new life into your life rituals. Find a new path, take a new journey, take control of your life. You are the governor of your life. You create it and direct it. Do so with harmony and discipline, and then you will know the true spirit of freedom. [55]

Bear

[Hibernation] often reflects a need to go deep within yourself, to have periods in your life when you can be more reclusive. ...Those who have a bear as a totem will find this cycle of semi-hibernation and reclusiveness during the winter very natural. They will also find that with the spring will come opportunities to act more assertively in regard to that which has been nursed through the winter months. ... All bears have a great fondness for honey...It is a reminder for those with this totem to go within to awaken the power, but only by bringing it out into the open and applying it will the honey of life be tasted. [56]

Raven

It is a bird of birth and death, and it is a bird of mysticism and magic. ...With raven, human and animal spirits intermingle and become as one. This is reflected in its deep, rich shiny black. In blackness, everything mingles until drawn forth, out into the light. Because of this, raven can help you shapeshift your life or your being. …[Their] creative life force can be used to work the magic of spiritual laws upon the physical plane. It can be used to go into the void and stir the energies to manifest that which you most need… If raven has come into your life, expect magic.[57]

Hmmm…maybe Spirit is telling me to ante up![58]

☙

And just to reinforce the message, I meet black bear up close and personal when I am hiking on a trail through the woods. I am moving swiftly, trying to get to see the waterfall at the end of the trail before the sun goes down. My head is down, watching the trail in front of me, navigating tree roots and rocks and brambles. Rounding a corner, I am suddenly upon the bear—and we both are startled. I breathe deeply, calm my energy, and back up slowly. Just in time, I erect my hand as a barrier to the charging youth behind me that has raced up the path and into this predicament. For several moments we hold our breath, wondering what happens next.

The bear trundles off into the brush, determining that there is no need for confrontation. A sigh of relief is breathed all around, and I am reminded of Spirit's message in the playing cards. Bear must be very important for me right now! Wow!!!

☙

On an especially relaxing morning during my stay in the Smoky Mountains, it is my birthday. My first thought upon waking is the beauty and peace of these woods, and how I could easily stay for another week. I could certainly stay for another couple of days. But something is tugging at me. That something begins with the letter Z. I realize he is only 3 hours away, and I want to see him.

"Go back to sleep Kerri," I direct myself.

Another three hours later I wake up again, and again, the desire is strong to see Z. *Sigh.* I text him a message that I am close, and would he be interested in a visitor albeit it is mid-week. I go back to sleep.

It is mid-afternoon, and I have apparently chosen to spend my birthday lolling about in my tent, alternating between sleeping and reading and staring at trees stretching above me.

Beep!

I check my message. "When will you be here? I'll tell the door man you're coming, and I will be there as soon as dinner with my boss is over."

It's on. I hope I'm ready for this.

ℨ

The elevator buzzes open and I am wandering around his apartment floor, moving left because I think I remember that's the way to go, and then realizing I was wrong. I'm heading back the other direction when he calls. "Are you here? The doorman says you took the elevator…" I laugh, saying I got turned around, and as I round the corner I see him. There he is. Z.

I'm sure I am a sight to see with my pink suitcase and journey drum and earthy appeal from spending days in the woods, outside of civilization. *Don't get crazy*, I tell myself as I greet him with a smile and a hug.

Hours later we are talking on his sofa, and his dog MuMu has cuddled up next to me with her roly-poly belly and black freckles and velvety soft curly black ears. "She doesn't normally do that," Z says.

I know.

I so love talking to Z, telling him all the stories of my adventures and hearing his quirky comments and wise insights. Hours pass that feel like minutes. I marvel that we are just enjoying each other's company; that I am not repeating my past mistakes. I'm not pressuring him to confess his feelings, or tell me how I'm perfect for him, or validate me in any way. I'm simply enjoying being with him.

And then as he is brushing his teeth, he says "Did you notice that I didn't offer you any wine? That we just had water and talked?" In fact, I did notice this. It means that Z listened to me when I told him I thought he was disconnected, that he was using alcohol to shut down his feelings, to numb himself from the possibility of feeling love. I remember when I told him this. I was feeling so frustrated by his reserve, by the walls he erected between us with his constant response to my expressions of love: "I hear you talking…"

When we sleep that night, we are sharing his bed as friends, jammies and all. I get to stretch my arms around that coastal brown bear as I sleep safe and sound in his den. I kiss him on his t-shirt, right where his shoulder blades meet.

I love you Z

The next morning he is up and making coffee and preparing for a day of work. He works from home, so it seems it is not inconvenient that I am there lingering after breakfast. But to be courteous to his space and concentration, I tell him I am happy to stay another day, since I am enjoying our time together, or I can mosey on home, whatever works for his schedule. He pauses while he considers this and says "I'd like you to stay if you want to. I'm enjoying having you here." I smile the biggest smile ever. "Ok!"

I gather up my spiritual reading that I've been meaning to do, and while he works, I read and write in my journal. We pass the day this way, in harmony in separate pursuits, and to me it feels natural.

After he is done with work, it is time to take MuMu for a trundle around the block. You can't really call it a walk with her; it's more like a trundle with her belly swaying back and forth as she moves. The end-of-work whistle blowing signals to me that it's time to connect, so I start telling Z all the interesting things I read during the day while he worked and participated in endless conference calls and suddenly he stops.

"Do you have any awareness of the people around you at all and how they might be feeling?"

I stop in my tracks and look him squarely in the eyes, and in my most authentic-*ness*, without any self-judgment or embarrassment, I genuinely admit the possibility that I don't. "Hmmm. I guess I'm not aware of how you're feeling. So can you use words and tell me what's going on with you? I'm not a mind-reader but I'm happy to listen, and to give you space if you need it."

Wow. I just had a moment of potential confrontation with someone I love, and it's ok. I stood my ground without fear or anger or insecurity or embarrassment. Yay!

So we walk in silence and after a while he says "I want to talk with you Pink because you're here and I miss you, and I want to spend time. I guess I'm just grumpy after a full day at work."

I smile. "It's ok Z. I understand. There's time tonight to talk. Right now, we can just be."

છ

Our time together is over too soon, and I must head back to Austin, to my family, to my new full-time job. Z walks me down to the garage to my car, and hugs me goodbye. He is walking away, and hesitates, looking back at me.

I hope I will see him again.

"Go! You're late!" I say and laugh. His conference call is about to start. I watch him smile as he turns and jogs back up the ramp to the elevator.

I'll miss you Z

All the way home, 15 hours in the car from Atlanta to Austin, I have space and time to contemplate all the twists and turns of my journey to and from the Smoky Mountains.

So I pick my heart up,
And start running from love,
As I'm searching for somebody new...
I just gravitate back to you.

What is so perplexing is that I am so sure of my feelings, but I absolutely do not have any clear cut answers or decisions or directions beyond heading home, reconnecting with my children, and starting my job.

I'm bothered that I am 43 and my life is entirely up in the air. According to society, I should be settled happily in a comfortable marriage and looking forward to retirement. Instead, I have upended my life completely, and I have no idea where my path will lead.

I notice my thoughts like a bystander, outright dismissing some as false and fear-generated. I realize that trust is a huge issue for me because I learned during my early childhood that knowing what you're doing is incredibly vital to safety, to quality of life and to my very existence.

I learned as a child that when you don't know what you're doing, and things don't go the way you expect, the result is that bad things happen to the people you love, and to you.

My ego mind is stepping it up. But so am I. I trust that the Universe is a joyful place that provides everything I need to be happy. My experience right now is HAPPINESS. I trust that I can have this happiness without knowing anything more about it than that it makes me happy right now.

Suggestions

Practice "Don't Know" Mind! Unless you are some kind of swami, you really don't know what comes next, or why events are rolling out the way they are in your life. All you can do is pay attention to the experiences you are having, and try not to label them or make projections about what these experiences _mean_ or what will happen next. "Don't know" mind gets to the heart of what Eckhart Tolle talks about: Be in the moment. Allow the moment to occur without having to control or understand or predict it.

Expect Waves! You are afloat on the sea of life. Expect to be tossed about by waves. It is an essential paradox that humans want stability and predictability, but live in an entirely unpredictable world where change is the only constant. Be kind to your human condition.

Create a Pause! When you react strongly to a situation, chances are you are threatened by it at a deep level. This situation may challenge your inner Jenga structure. Allow a pause before you respond; allow yourself the time to investigate the agreement inside of you that is being challenged.

Measure Success with Your Inner Pendulum! Think of yourself as a pendulum. Your 'center' is where lies your divinity, your essential nature, and your equilibrium and peace. Life's events will swing you out in one direction, and gravitational pull will launch you naturally the opposite direction with equal force. A pendulum will swing either direction with lesser and lesser pull until eventually it rests back at center. When life tosses you an unexpected challenge, how quickly can you get return to center, to peace, to equilibrium, to acceptance?

Remember the Spiral! It's an important visual to remember that our life progresses as an upwards spiral that moves outwards slightly at each circuitous path, allowing us to see all the times before that we met our personal nemesis and responded to it. Having the view of these past encounters enables us to choose a new response, something not yet attempted. The challenges will continue; Spirit will keep pressing us forward to resolve our inner landscape of hurdles. The only thing that can change is our <u>response</u> to the challenge.

Quotes

"Focusing energy from a place of inner alignment and truth is like being the river rushing across the stones."
— Kerri Hummingbird Lawnsby

"Nothing binds you except your thoughts; nothing limits you except your fear; and nothing controls you except your beliefs." — Marianne Williamson

"We're in some kind of fantasy projection that is taking us away from the present moment." — Jim Garrison

"There is a fine line between humble and ashamed. Humble opens the door to God. Shame closes it. If we move through our lives riddled with shame, we have a much harder time believing in our inherent magnificence. Unfortunately, many of us do not have self-love handed to us. We have to forge it ourselves in the fires of life. This is the work of our lives, recognizing the Godself sleeping at the core of our being."
— Jeff Brown

"Many people who are going through the early stages of the awakening process are no longer certain of what their outer purpose is. What drives the world no longer drives them. Seeing the madness of our civilization so clearly, they may feel somewhat alienated from the culture around them. Some feel that they inhabit a no-man's land between two worlds. They are no longer run by the ego, yet the arising awareness has not yet become fully integrated into their lives." —Eckhart Tolle

"Life has a funny way of teaching us lessons. When there is something you need to learn, something that you need to work on, the same situation will continue to repeat itself until you either learn your lesson or find a healthy way of dealing with that particular issue....A good way of recognizing patterns in your life is by listening to your feelings, your intuition. I've found that when I am involved in a pattern, my emotions run a bit stronger, kind of like a warning from my subconscious mind to pay attention to what's happening."
—Maria Cristina McDonald

Living for Me

After starting my full-time job, I realize I have a new opportunity: I can buy a home. I've always been a homeowner, since I was 23, but it was with the combined power of my ex-husband's income. When I started consulting, our mortgages and refinances did not list my income because it was too complicated to use self-employed earnings—even though I often made as much or more than my husband. As a Smith College graduate, it was a thorn in my side to be listed as a homemaker on our applications.

Now that I have the ability to secure a mortgage, I am ready to find a home where I can begin the journey of my independent life. I don't know how long it will be until I have a partner to share my life, so it makes perfect sense to just proceed as if I will be alone.

I am excited and nervous, and curious about what my new life will look like. I am grateful to even have this opportunity to buy a home of my own, to build a comfortable and secure life as a single mother.

I do some searching online and quickly determine a few criteria: I do not want to be in over my head on this mortgage; I want a friendly safe neighborhood with lots of kids; I want to be as close as possible to the kids' schools. There are not many neighborhoods with homes in my desired price range that also have the warm appeal I seek. My realtor takes me to several different neighborhoods and we look, but I do not love any of these homes.

Frustrated, I look again online. Somehow I discover a neighborhood I did not notice the first time I looked. It's perfect with its vintage style clapboard homes—painted blue, yellow, sage, taupe—and white picket fences. It reminds me of where I have lived in New England and California, all at once. I love this neighborhood. I identify several homes and we go looking.

I like these homes a great deal, but I am not in love until I face this adorable blue cottage with a bay window in the front, and peaked roofs on the second level. Stepping into the house, I feel tremendous love surrounding me, hovering in the air like the smell of cookies out of the oven.

For some reason, the upstairs loft in this home is bright and airy, filled with light. It is just like another home, that has exactly the same layout, but the light in this house is *different*.

I decide to make an offer. Back at home, I gather my children and I tell them the exciting news. I take out my drum and begin drumming to Spirit for help, for guidance in securing this new home. My sons chant along with me as we sing the home's address, and how we want it to be our new home. We giggle and chant in our excitement, and we are filled with hope!

Just then my realtor calls and says there is already on offer on the table that has gone back and forth for 3 days now. She is sorry that the home will probably not be open for an offer. I tell her not to worry. I know this house is mine. Tell the other realtor my offer will come if the counter offer is not accepted.

I go into my room with my drum. This time, it is a sacred drum meditation, a communion with Spirit, seeking guidance for this house that I simply know is my home. I *feel* it. I journey as I drum, envisioning living in my home, and hosting dinner parties with friends.

At some point in my journey my grandma and grandpa, long deceased, are in my dream. Grandma is exclaiming over how cute the kitchen and pantry are, how excited she is for this new home for me and my children. They hug me goodbye, and just then…*magic* happens. Outside the back kitchen window I see a Technicolor hummingbird float and hover outside the window, like it is swimming in a rainbow sea, and I exclaim "Wow!" I know this is Spirit because I am not anticipating this experience at all.

When I look up hummingbird in my Animal Spirit guide, I see Spirit has indeed spoken…

"You need to be very flexible with the twists and turns your life will take in the next few days."

Even more interesting, I discover that if Hummingbird is your power animal:

"You're fiercely independent, and if anyone threatens that independence you're prepared to take flight. You're full of joy, generally have a positive outlook, and affect others in this way. It's crucial for your health and sanity to find work that allows you to be outdoors as much as possible.

You're extremely sensitive, drawn to those who are light and positive, while shying away from anyone with harsh or negative energies. You confound others with your ability to go from being passionate to cool, or intimate to emotionally distant, in the blink of an eye."

I know that Spirit has just given me my name: Hummingbird. It is my very nature to dart around from flower to flower, fully saturating myself in every experience, heart and wings fluttering at a mile a minute. I am joy and light.

And apparently, this home is where my nature will flourish because 45 minutes later the counter offer is rejected, and now the sellers have an opportunity to consider my offer. I make a generous one, and send over a card with my artwork on it. I tell the sellers how much I feel the love in their home, and how I hope they will decide to let me be the new owner. Since the wife is a seamstress, and creative, I think she will be excited to pass the house to another artist. In fact, she is, and the sellers accept my offer within a day. They accept my offer even though it comes with the stipulation that my mortgage will not be approved for 50 days because I must wait to receive a full month of paychecks from my employer for the credit approval.

Spirit is very generous indeed!

ℭ

I head to California to the office for a visit after my job starts, and it is an opportunity to reconnect with friends. But I have one evening free, and I decide it would be fun to go on a date. So I login to the dating site and fire off a couple of messages to local men.

Stephen answers my invitation, and we make a plan to meet after work at my hotel. When he arrives, I have an instant attraction for him, and he for me. As we are talking, getting to know each other by sharing our stories of past relationships and failed marriages, it is dawning on me that meeting Stephen is not coincidence. As it turns out, Stephen's first wife, brother, and several serious relationships have all been diagnosed with borderline personality disorder. In fact, he has been seriously traumatized by his relationships with his BPD loved ones.

When I tell him that I have been diagnosed BPD, he literally jumps backwards. He is instantly wary of me, and absolutely shocked and taken aback. He cannot believe that I am borderline personality because I do not seem like it at all to him. I feel there is some serious significance to our meeting, and I tell him so. Perhaps he needs to know that people can heal themselves of BPD, can overcome it and transform their lives. I share my story of healing with energy and shamanic practices, and he is listening and fascinated, albeit still wary.

By the end of the evening, we are energetically and emotionally very close. We end up spending the night together making love, and I feel it is some tremendous healing that has taken place between two people traumatized by BPD, each from the opposite perspective of this debilitating disorder.

Spirit is slapping me in the face with a mission. Somehow, I think I'm meant to help people who suffer with borderline personality, and the people who love them. This mission feels immense, to the edge of my comfort zone and beyond. Am I ready for this journey?

ଔ

Back at home after my trip, I have begun feeling the familiar obsession for Stephen, the insecurity that comes when text messages are not returned within the window of my comfort zone. In honesty and respect for this man, I confess it.

"I am feeling uneasy with our contact.
Like I want your attention too much."

He knows BPD well, and his own limits. He responds.

"This doesn't sound good Kerri.
It makes me nervous."

I know I have a choice. I want to prove to him that BPD can be cured, that I can be symptom-free from all the work I have done. But this is not the truth. What is true is that I can be aware of my triggers and choose to respond differently to them, to respond in ways that do not hurt the people I care about. But I do not know that I will ever truly be *free* of my triggers.

"I am letting you go. Take care."

He responds.

"Thank you Kerri."

I feel that I have moved deeper into my authenticity. I have been honest with myself about what I can and cannot handle. I have saved myself the struggle of trying to project myself as bigger or more capable than I really am at the moment, and it feels—not like giving up on myself—but like loving myself enough to walk away from a challenge that is not necessary for my life.

❧

I have begun taking a course at church called the *Seven Keys to the Kingdom*. Its goal is to increase the prosperity in your life, and the prosperity I want to increase is *love*.

I learn about true abundance and how to cultivate it by implementing the seven keys. In many ways, these teachings are another window into the same truths I have learned in Spirit Paths. It is essential to examine my limiting beliefs, to unclutter my life, and to let go of the past and forgive myself and others.

Fulfilling the mission of uncluttering my life, I begin going through my closet and pulling out all clothing and shoes I have not worn in the past year. I put it into bags for Good Will. I have 7 bags of donations for Good Will when I finish.

Now I am purposeful about uncluttering my life. I go through my drawers and throw away all of my old lingerie. I realize these garments are saturated with negative juju—all my past love experiences are held inside these frilly outfits, and I no longer want them, or the men I shared them with, to be part of my story.

As I am cleaning my closet, I discover a large white garment bag at the back of the closet and I pull it out. *My wedding dress.* I unzip the bag and pull out the dress. It is still as beautiful as it was the day I wore it. I am filled with sadness. It is time to apologize to this dress, to the young woman who wore it all those years ago, and to forgive myself for ending my marriage so that my soul had space to grow.

I fill my seashell with white sage and light it. White smoke fills my room as I move about, lifting the smoke into recesses in my closet. I shake my rattle to break up negative energy and dislodge it from my belongings, from my space, from my wedding dress.

I repeat this mantra:

> *I'm sorry. Please forgive me. I love you. Thank you.*

Images from my wedding ceremony, feelings from my youth, memories from my marriage, all swirl around inside me as I perform this cleansing ritual and release the sadness welling up inside of me. Regret and anger pass through me and out as I continue to chant:

> *I'm sorry. Please forgive me. I love you. Thank you.*

I see the young woman I was the day I became a wife, filled with promise and hope and joy and love. Believing the honey of life would be tasted.

> *I'm sorry. Please forgive me. I love you. Thank you.*

I see the young mother, overwhelmed with the stresses of caring for an infant, feeling incapable of comforting the wailing baby, not knowing what to do, not feeling like a good mother at all.

I'm sorry. Please forgive me. I love you. Thank you.

I see a woman running from herself, from her fears, from her truth. I see a woman staying so busy she has no time to consider that this life she has built is tearing her apart from the inside.

I'm sorry. Please forgive me. I love you. Thank you.

I see a woman finally choosing herself, choosing time and space to heal, choosing quiet and contemplation, choosing to leave behind all she has built as the dream of her life to start on a journey to a destination unknown.

I'm sorry. Please forgive me. I love you. Thank you.

Exhausted after what feels like hours, I lay my empty body across my bed and sleep peacefully.

ରଷ

A year ago I started my journey to me. From the outside, my life looks like a wreckage of relationships started and ended, communities left, creativity put on hold, binfuls of empty wine bottles.

But my inner garden is shaping up nicely. I value and love myself. A year ago I didn't know what that meant. Now I do. It means I am willing to let go of anything and anyone that does not help my garden grow. The essentials needed for my garden—light, love, acceptance and peace—are all right here inside of me.

ରଷ

I return to Gerry for shamanic healing work. I feel like it is time for yet another transformational shift, for letting go of another layer of my past. After drumming and consulting spirit, Gerry feels it is right to perform some Reiki energy work. So I lie on his massage table, and close my eyes as he starts meditating. I am feeling the flow of energy as he works, but at some point I realize I am tense, I am resisting. I explore this resistance and discover that Gerry is pulling something upwards and out of me, something I do not need, and I am resisting it. I encourage myself to simply let go, to allow whatever this is to be removed from me. As soon as I make this decision, I feel it leave and Gerry flicks it to the ground. Afterwards, Gerry and I compare notes and realize we are describing the same experience. Indeed, a layer of me that is no longer needed has been lifted up and out, and returned to Mother Earth. I feel lighter and freer.

Gerry decides it is time to return my soul part to my energy body. He takes the crystal and blows the little soul piece contained within it into the middle of my chest. I feel as if I have been reunited with the part of me that was lost when I was a year and a half. Gerry reminds me to keep it safe inside my body, safe inside my being, or else this little soul part may flee again.

The next morning, I find myself absentmindedly putting double the brown sugar in my oatmeal. Ha!! Just like a two year old to want more sugar.

଼

I continue to date, but the experiences are frustrating for me. I keep dating men that cannot commit to returning a phone call. There is a philosophy that the Universe simply mirrors back to you what you are; with this scenario, I figure I must be broken inside.

I meet with Chrispy and he dissuades me from this line of reasoning. He encourages me to remember that the challenges will continue, but it is how I respond to each challenge that defines my character. I need to hear this lesson again.

I refocus my intent on deriving my happiness from ME. There is a deep shadow over my joy, entrenched, and I have been working so hard at opening and releasing that it is losing its grip. I am ready to beat it and allow the sunshine in.

଼

The day has finally come to close on my house. When I am signing for my mortgage, as the only homeowner, I feel so proud of myself. It is empowering to provide for myself and my children, to have my income and capabilities be the only justification for this mortgage.

In the days that follow, I prepare my new nest by painting all the walls in the living room and bedroom with my friend John. It is empowering to transform this house into my home.

I pack my things into boxes and hire a moving company to move my belongings. On moving day, three burly guys show up to move my things. And they do it with finesse. One man hoists my queen pillow-top mattress with one arm and carries it out of my apartment and onto the truck. Hot dang moving day is fun!

On the first night in my new home, I have a moment to notice 'aloneness'. I am getting more comfortable with being alone, but I am not yet fully adjusted to it. I am happy to be in my new home, but I do cry a bit with the loneliness of not having 'someone'.

෯

Every night and weekend I unpack boxes, putting my things away in newly designated places in my home. The clutter in my house and garage becomes less as things find their places.

A month has passed and it feels like two weeks. On the day my Spirit Paths friends will come to my home to bless it, I am scurrying about making preparations. Out on my front porch, I realize that the hanging plants are dead. "That does not bode well for a home blessing," I smile to myself, and I head to Home Depot for some new plants. Upon entering the Garden Center, I immediately notice a handsome man perusing plants, mostly because he looks up as I walk in and beams a magnificent smile. He literally glows with energy, and I am drawn into him.

"Plants!" I remind myself of the mission at hand. I am wandering about the aisles for a bit before I realize I'm in the sunshine plant area, and what I likely need are shade plants since these fellas will be hanging on my shady porch. But as I make my way over there, I notice that handsome man again. He is looking at a beautiful plant with dark leaves and purple blossoms, and I realize I love this plant. "Is this cliché?" I ask myself, but then shake my head and speak to him. "Isn't that plant lovely? What is it?"

We strike up a conversation that flows effortlessly. Before long I am giving him my number for a later date, and after he texts me, I am entering his contact information. *David*.

❧

Later in the evening, Gerry has arrived along with several of my classmates from Spirit Paths. We are settling into some drumming for a journey to establish me as the new owner of this home, and to tap into the spiritual realm of the land on which my home sits.

The neighborhood was built on ranch land with a rich history that began with Tonkawa and Comanche Indians blessing the area as hunting grounds. Once settlers moved in and claimed the territory there were bloody reprisals. Far more recently, Ku Klux Klan hunted and hanged black people from the trees on this land. Powerful human experiences have soaked into this earth, leaving an energetic trace hard to ignore. So saturated with spirit is this land, that word spread far enough to garner the attention of Travel Channel's *The Dead Files*, resulting in the *Surrounded* episode.

As our journey proceeds, Gerry makes contact with a spirit Shaman who welcomes me. He confirms what I have suspected from my own experiences of the house and land: many spirits pass through this area, not dwelling for long, but nonetheless here.

I welcome the spirit beings who pass on the land, but caution that my home is a safe place for me, my boys, and my guests. If at any point my home feels unsafe, my offer to share space will be rescinded. For now, the spirit world greets me with a hearty Welcome.

❧

It is time for the weekend conference at my church, *'Be the Change'*, where I will be learning wisdom from Don Miguel Ruiz Jr., the son of the author of 'The Four Agreements' which I studied in Spirit Paths for months.

My first workshop of the weekend is with HeatherAsh Amara of the Toltec Center of Creative Intent (TOCI). She is teaching us on Friday night about the fire walk, an ancient tradition since humanity first discovered fire. While the fire burns the wood, she teaches us that we make agreements about how life is since we are little children. And some of those agreements we make are based on our perceptions, which may or may not be accurate. As adults, we have a choice to see reality as we experience it, to choose how we view the world.

About fifty people are gathered around the smoldering hot coals that have been spread over two layers of sod, and then heaped into glowing piles at either side of the pathway down which those who wish to, will walk. The pathway across which we will walk is covered with a layer of embers that are glowing red and orange, alerting us to the immense heat held inside.

We begin to chant and clap, and as I stare at the glowing remnants of the fire, I start to feel an awakening of the primeval, the ancient within me. I am in awe as the first person crosses the burning pathway, cheering and exclaiming at the other side with the accomplishment.

I am paying attention to my body. We have been instructed that we do not walk until our bodies urge us to walk. But when the lady next to me walks, and I am reminded of how afraid she was to walk and that she is much older than me, I tell myself to go. Of course I can do this!

I steel my nerves, and imagine a safe passage across the fiery embers, and putting one foot in front of the other, I cross. My feet tingle with the sensation, my heart races with adrenaline, and when I reach the other side I am cheered by those waiting. Wow! I made it!

I have been kissed by the fire, I can feel where the fire has more deeply touched the soles of my feet, but I have not been burned. I almost cannot believe it.

My mind starts rationalizing all the reasons why what just happened cannot possibly have happened.

The fire must not be real.
They must wait for it to get to be a certain temperature before they let you walk.
If I walk again, I'll surely be burned next time.
I just got lucky.

As my doubt grows, the tingling in my feet intensifies. I remember what I was told about being kissed by fire, and I breathe deeply. I imagine breathing the fire up into myself from the bottom of my feet into my very being. As I do this, the sensation subsides and eventually goes away entirely. I am back in the moment, watching the fire, clapping, chanting. I realize I must need to walk again to learn this lesson about false beliefs versus actual experience.

Then HeatherAsh stops the chanting and drumming and clapping. She instructs that now we will be silent. Those who wish to cross the fire in silence will approach the glowing pathway, utter a word for us all to repeat, and then cross the burning embers.

My body immediately walks to the fire, pulled to it by a force greater than me. I pause at the beginning of the pathway and speak:

"I love myself"

As fifty people repeat my words, I float across the fire walk and something deep inside me clicks like a key in a lock: *I love myself.* The ground beneath my feet feels like soft dewy grass as I calmly place one tender foot in front of the other onto hot burning coals. I dream my way across the embers enveloped in a magical bubble of peace, and I do not feel the slightest bit of heat.

I marvel at my soft pink feet later that night after I have taken a hot bath that didn't feel nearly as hot as usual, thanks to the fire. I am amazed at my body, my spirit, and the Universe in which I dwell. I thought I understood fire.

Tonight I learned I do not know what I think I do. I must learn to practice 'don't know mind' because what I know is really a matter of what I *choose* to believe.

ℭ

Over the days following the fire, I notice a growing sensation of being watched when I move about my house. It is so strong, that sometimes I cautiously peer over my shoulder to see what is behind me, only to find there is nothing visual. Yet I can feel something there.

It is fall, and the weather is unseasonably warm, so I spend most days working from my back porch with my company laptop. One morning as I am sipping my coffee and reviewing emails, my normally mellow and quiet Daddy Dawg transforms into a growling, snarling, vicious beast with paws up on the left side of my chair, lunging at the empty space to my right. My heart starts pounding. I look to the emptiness and see nothing, then return gaze to Daddy who definitely believes what he is sensing is dangerous. I look back to the empty space and as calmly as I can, I say to it, whatever <u>it</u> is:

"You are scaring my dog.
You must now leave."

I feel a tingling and glowing sensation pass through my body and then, there is quiet. Daddy returns to normal and goes to lie down in the sunshine on the grass.

What just happened?

I call some *Spirit Paths* friends and I find out that apparently my light, my energy, has gotten very big from walking on fire and it has attracted attention. From what, I don't know. They recommend I shield my home with a special ceremony that I invent, the most important element of which is my clear intention that nothing is allowed in the space of my home without my permission.

So after a trip to the rock store to get some protective crystals, and the grocery store to get some Epsom salts and a compass, I am ready.

Starting in the East, I bury a cleansing crystal into the soil, pour some salt on top, and repeat my mantra three times in my mind.

I am the owner and protector of this property.
Any being wishing to stay must have as its
sole purpose increasing the Light, Love, Peace,
Beauty, and Joy of myself, my children and
my guests. If you have any other purpose
you must now leave and never return.

I move to the South and repeat this process, followed by West and North. On the way to North I have to hop my fence which I am positive any watching neighbors are noting as pure lunacy on my part. Especially when I do it two more times: I have to make three rounds around my property repeating this protective shielding. So…ok…I look insane.

Later in the evening as I am tucked into bed, I do a mental scan of my protective shield, imagining it as a golden sphere of light encompassing my home and yard above, below, and around. I have awareness that there is a tiny gap in this shield to the West. I don't know how I know, I just do. So I pray. I pray to my angels, to my spirit guides, to God, to lock that shield down tight. I feel it fasten and seal, and I hear something bump against it like a ball bouncing off a wall.

It howls.

ॐ

My home feels so much lighter and safer the next morning. But I am still a bit rattled from my experiences over the last few days. It is one thing to have the idea that there is spirit moving in the world unseen. It is another thing entirely to *experience* it with your own senses.

Later in the morning, over coffee with Chrispy, I am recounting my experiences and he is listening avidly. To tell these stories to someone and not be committed to an insane asylum is very encouraging. Although, I have to remind myself that Chrispy is extremely open-minded.

"Pay attention to your experience," Chrispy advises. "Do what feels right for you. There is no handbook on Life. There is only your path."

Following our session I meet a friend for lunch. He has been struggling with his ex-wife's lifestyle choices for quite a while; since I've known him actually. And it seems, from her latest series of inappropriate conduct with my friend's children nearby, he might have cause to be concerned. I am listening and offering whatever wisdom I can to my friend as we eat.

Suddenly, I feel a different energetic, a weightier presence, descend upon me, press into me, and I am saying things to my friend that are not coming from me, but from Spirit.

My friend is staring at me in disbelief as we both come into the shared awareness that something larger than ourselves is communicating through me to him.

When it passes, there is silence, followed by giddy nervousness. "Wow," he says. I nod. "Wow."

On the way home I am saturated by emotions I know do not belong to me, but to the spiritual presence that was moved to communicate heart-felt urgings to my friend through me. I release them, knowing they do not belong to me. But I am left feeling like an empty shell. And in this emptiness, I need comfort.

I text David, and tell him "I need to be held."

We have been sharing coffee on my back porch for several weeks, discoursing on a number of spiritual topics including my recent experiences. David is trained as a minister, and is well versed in Christian belief. He has quoted me numerous passages from the Bible that caution against the sort of contact I have been experiencing from Spirit. While he has offered scriptural wisdom, however, David has been anything but judgmental about my stories. David knows I do not subscribe to a single spiritual belief.

When he arrives, I greet him at the door and fall into his arms. I am so thankful to be held by someone who understands the world in which I have been walking. He is patient, and kind, and understanding.

There is an immense attraction here, and I feel the synergy of our energies every time we meet. However, I have started to question whether he feels the same way, although he has told me he does, because it's really not progressing. He only comes for coffee, and we talk and work on our laptops, and then he leaves. It's strange that it's not progressing towards a real date.

On this occasion, I am being held by this man, comforted by him, and in closer physical contact than ever before. The energy begins to shift and attraction swells. I am moved to lift my face towards his and then his lips are on mine. We kiss passionately, relishing this first moment of intimacy. And then it is over and he releases me.

"We need to talk," he says. So we sit down and I have no idea what is coming. "I hope you can understand how difficult this is, given my beliefs." He pauses. "Kerri, I am still married. I've told my wife I want a divorce, weeks before I ever met you, but for now, I'm still married."

Everything makes sense now. It has felt to me like this relationship should be a rushing river, but instead it has been a gurgling creek. And now I know why. I am crushed. I allow the silence while I feel into what I need to say.

"I can understand your situation, David," I sigh. "But I can't walk this journey with you. You have to do this all on your own. It makes me so sad because I enjoy you so much. But I don't do well with anything other than straight up, open and available, relationships."

After he leaves, I cry. I feel like I'm being punished. I've done everything I can do to better myself, to heal, to forgive. Why would I be shown someone as wonderful as David, experience a connection like this, to have it be unavailable to me? Even if he gets a divorce next week, I know from my own journey that it will be a year or more before he is ready to love again. This is no short term prognosis.

As I allow the waves of emotion to pass over me, and through me, an awareness dawns that perhaps this encounter was a test of my character.

What am I willing to do for love?
Will I compromise myself, my morals, to have it?

ભ

At church on Sunday we have a guest speaker: Janet Connor who just published *The Lotus and the Lily*. Her talk is so inspiring, that I purchase her new book and her previous book, *Writing Down Your Soul*, which describes how to access wisdom from Spirit through journaling.

During her talk, she explains her revelation about the paradox of prosperity and how our focus on manifesting what we want (with teachings like *The Secret*) is backwards. Our focus first needs to be on tilling the soil so that we can then plant the seeds of our intentions.

I decide that this unique 30-day program is exactly what I need right now in my life. I buy the books, secure Janet's autograph as a good luck charm, and begin diving into the pages. First stop: my intention for starting this program.

After considering this question carefully, I retreat to my loft studio where I create a pastel artwork to represent the lush garden I want to achieve by cultivating my conditions. Then, I write my intention into this artwork:

Intention:
Liberate myself from pain and heaviness.
Step forward into a new CONSCIOUSNESS of playfulness, creativity and happiness.

ભ

I repeat this mantra every day while looking at the artwork as it hangs on my bedroom wall.

Suggestions

Listen to Spirit! When you receive messages from Spirit, in whatever form they come, pay attention to what is being conveyed. The appearance of Hummingbird in my journey dream was significant in giving me a way to better understand my own true nature. By observing a Hummingbird, I can understand myself and how I operate in the world. I am quick, I dart around from flower to flower, immersing myself fully and then darting off again to fully explore the next flower. My little heart beats so quickly and my wings flit at a mile a minute as I consume experience at a lightning pace. Knowing Hummingbird gives me a way of accepting my natural processes.

When Purpose Finds You, Accept the Challenge! We are often called to take selfless action so that healing can occur in the world. When I met Stephen, I knew I was being called to write about my story, to share my healing process with borderline personality disorder. I had a great deal of fear about this purpose. Largely because being absolutely truthful, which is what is needed for a book like this, I will forever close the door to part of my family.

Forgive! Forgiveness is essential for healing. We must forgive the loved ones who hurt us, and mostly, we must forgive ourselves. There are many ways to invite forgiveness, and you can invent your own methods. The Ho'oponopono prayer is an excellent meditation to do while holding in your mind and heart the person you want to forgive:

"I'm sorry. Please forgive me. I love you. Thank you."

Recapitulate! Recapitulation is another way to practice forgiveness...for yourself. Meditate on the situation you need to forgive, visualize it and experience the emotions...then change the story. Make it how you wish it would have been. Feel how good it would be to have this different version of the story be true. One recapitulation I did for myself was around my first stepfather hitting me when I was 3 because I touched his guitar. In my mind, I rewrote the story so that he bought me my own guitar, sized just right for me, and then taught me to play it. We played guitar together and sang, and that felt really good. In real life, I bought myself a beautiful Eastman parlor guitar and began lessons.

Fire Walking! Walking across hot burning embers is a powerful lesson in how our minds can construct reality based on agreements we make as children, before we are able to think consciously. Getting to the other side of the fire walk unscathed is powerful. It means that any notion in your head, any absolute truth you think you know, is called into question. Walking multiple times across the fire is equally as powerful. It teaches you that each experience is its own moment in time, and will be like no other. Nothing in this world can be predicted, and yet, as humans we are constantly seeking predictability. Fire teaches us to stay in the present moment and observe it for what it is, experientially, without the mind. Fire teaches us to live with our hearts.

Let Go! Life is a process of letting go so that room can be made for the new in our lives. Clean out your closets and let go of clothes you are not wearing. Clean out your emotional closet and let go of whatever past experience you are holding onto that no longer serves you in this moment. Let go of old versions of you that do not fit the life you want to step into. Let go so you can make space.

Quotes

"...the Universe always moves in to fill a vacuum. Dig a hole on the beach and the wet sand slides in to reclaim it. Suck the air from your mouth, and your cheeks collapse to fill the void. Plow under a meadow and nature immediately begins to replant it. You cannot move something out of the way and maintain emptiness for very long. The universe abhors a vacuum and will always move to fill it." — David Owen Ritz [59]

"The process of recapitulation is more than just remembering and allowing yourself to be overwhelmed by memories. By going fully into the experience and feelings, to completely release them through personal choice, you can finally take back the power lost in those moments. You can also 're-script' the event—change the ending—and turn the trauma into an act of power." — Gerry Starnes, M.Ed. [60]

"One of the first things we learn is that fire burns. When you first see someone walk on fire, or you walk yourself, this fundamental law shatters. And suddenly the world is full of open possibilities. If it wasn't true that fire burns all the time, what else that you have been telling yourself might also not be true? This is the gift and lesson of firewalking: by challenging our beliefs we open up our perspective and begin to take responsibility for creating something more expanded and powerful with our lives." — HeatherAsh Amara

"When you overcome your senses, when you understand that you are not bound by the chains of your past—when you live a life that is greater than your body, your environment, and time—all things are possible. The universal intelligence that animates the existence of all things will both surprise and delight you. It wants nothing more than to provide you with access to all you want. In short, when you change your mind, you change your life." —Dr. Joe Dispenza [61]

Slithering across dirt, rocks, debris
The old skin tore loose revealing unknown
Discarded as the empty husk
Of a life well lived and outgrown

Now awareness stirs from within
Unrelenting focus undeniably pinpointing
That which is, and is not, Self
Fearlessly, then, freeing all that is clinging

Closer to the surface, joyfully I rise
Seeing newly through my own eyes
No longer submerged under facade
Rather, I am shining, radiant, and wise

Feathered wings magically appear
Hearkening a mystical Spirit flight
My soul is ready for whatever comes
Willingly merging with vast glowing light

— Kerri Hummingbird

Trust in Love

A few weeks later, I have been sticking to the tasks in *The Lotus and the Lily*, but I have not been able to stick to my resolve in giving up David. I know it's wrong to keep in contact with this committed man, feeling the way I feel about him, but the feeling I get when I am with him is addictive. As with most borderline personality disorder people, boundaries are difficult for me to put into place and enforce.

I am in personal conflict on the David issue, and at Journey Circle I purposefully request guidance from Spirit to help me find the right path. The message I receive during my lucid journey dream is:

Trust in Love.
Feelings are more true than thoughts.

I take this to mean that I should trust in the way I feel about David. Even though he is married, and is unavailable to me, I should trust in the way I feel about him because somehow it will all work out in the end.

I am on a high with this revelation. I can believe this story because I want to believe this story. But I know what happens next because I have experienced this before. I want so much to have the love, that when it is unavailable I lash out.

It happens that he cannot come to visit when he says he will. In this instant, all of the times that he asked me not to text back because he would be home with his wife, all of the times that he did not come as promised, all of the disappointments collect and become one united front of **NO**! And I send him away.

"Do not contact me again until
you are a single available man."

I am, of course, miserable. I take a jog to move the energy. During my jog I ask Spirit for wisdom. What do I need to do better with these romantic relationships? What am I doing wrong? And Spirit answers:

Be skeptical. Trust and love are earned.

Now I remember Z: "I hear you talking, we will see." And I fully understand.

> *The greatest test of character*
> *is walking away from your heart's desire*
> *when the timing is not right.*

ভ

I feel like I am on the same spiral, repeating the same patterns. But this time, I learn a different lesson because I have been doing my homework. I have been studying and listening to Spirit. I take out my journal and ask Spirit:

> *"Have I understood the message from Journey Circle? Is there a different*
> *way to see it? Have I lost an opportunity to trust love by sending David*
> *away?"*

And Spirit guides my hand to write:

> *"No...you have acted wisely.*
> *It is not the right time for this love to manifest.*
> *You have taken correct action."*

And so I think about this paradox. Trust love. And yet, turn love away. And I think about Buddha's teaching: "When conditions are sufficient, there will be a manifestation."

So I wonder if conditions are not sufficient for romantic love, might they be sufficient for other kinds of love? Because my experience of love with David was that my heart felt love. If my heart felt love, that means conditions were sufficient for it to feel love. Therefore, if my heart can feel love, then what other kinds of love might be more fulfilling right now, at this present moment in my life?

My next prayer becomes:

> *"Spirit, please help me become aware of other ways I might experience love*
> *than the one way I have been seeking of romantic love with a man."*

For the first time, I am opening myself to the Universe to show me what kind of love will be most fulfilling for my soul at this time in my

136

experience of life. I am not telling Spirit what I want to receive; I am asking for guidance, and accepting that 'conditions' might not be sufficient for what I think I want. In fact, what I think I want (love from a man) might be the furthest thing from what is best for me at this point in time.

The answer comes quickly with a rap on the door and my son Garrett entering my room simply because he wants to hug me and tell me he loves me. He leaves after I oblige, and I continue to write in my journal only to be interrupted a second time with my son Tanner who has felt compelled to hug his mommy and tell her he loves her. *Ahhhh…*Now I see.

Just to be sure I understand the message, however, the phone rings a moment later and it is my friend Marques calling to check on me. Marques is everything I want in a man—intellectual, spiritual, creative, fun, and chocolate—but he prefers men. While I am telling Marques of my recent man adventures and lessons from Spirit, my friend John texts me to check up on me and see how things are going. John and I have been friends a very long time, since our oldest children were in kindergarten. We have been friends through the ending of both of our marriages, and supported each other through many shifts. I'm still talking with Marques when another text comes in from my friend Lindsay from Spirit Paths who is touching base to make sure I'm doing well. Meanwhile, Daddy Dawg has jumped up on the bed and is kissing my face with wild abandon.

Spirit is making it very clear that I have many, many ways to experience love in my life if only I am willing to open myself to the possibilities. Silently, I thank Spirit and acknowledge the message has been received.

ॐ

Since before my son Garrett was born, I have wanted to visit the Mayan ruins near Cancun, Mexico, and experience these ancient monuments built by a lost civilization. Fear prevented me from traveling there while I was married; my ex-husband was dissuaded by tales of tourists abducted and robbed, or even worse, tortured, raped and killed.

In the world I have chosen to believe, the world of Spirit and Universal protection, I decide to stop saying "I always wanted to" and just do it. I book a plane ticket to Cancun, a taxi to Tulum, and a beach-side cabana for one.

In preparation for this trip, I have to do the activity that most women loathe: I have to shop for a swimsuit. I know already that I absolutely have no interest in a bikini, or in looking like a Barbie. Had enough of that, thank you! I also do not want to look like a frump. In the dressing room, I have to face 3-way mirrors that point out all the ways I have not been paying attention to my physique. I most definitely could stand to lose 20 pounds.

I decide I would like to turn this experience inside out; I want to have fun on the eve of my vacation rather than torment myself for not being good enough. So I rewrite my story and post it on Facebook for my friends, and myself:

I have lived decadently with pizza, wine and chocolate and earned sexy voluptuous curves. Kapow!

This new story brings a smile to my face, and I am able to find two new swimsuits that accent my features and mask my indulgences.

After I have packed and it is near time to go to sleep on the eve of my departure, I pick up my drum for a special meditation. In my darkened room, I beat a heart rhythm on my journey drum, and after a while my mind starts painting pictures with messages from Spirit. I see eagle soaring high where land meets sky in an arc. I fly with eagle above the earth, so high it feels we are in orbit around the planet. It is liberating to fly so high. A new sound emerges from my drumming; it is as if a reed instrument is accompanying the drumbeat, and at moments, I hear the cooing of a Dove. I keep drumming to elongate the mystical experience of this entrancing concert until I am so sleepy I must put my drum down and lay my head to rest.

CB

Flying to Cancun, I gaze out the window at the low clouds as they cast inky shadows over the rippled waters. A rainbow of colors—golden to rose to indigo—paint this watery portrait.

When I arrive, I am diverted by salespeople trying to book tours, but once I realize what is being communicated through broken English (since I only know enough Spanish to find the bathroom and a drink of water), I make my way out of the airport to the driver who awaits me.

I take the passenger seat up front so I can talk to this man and find out more about this part of the country. I enjoy the fact that we are driving on a two-lane highway past acres and acres of undeveloped forest. It is refreshing to not see a Target or Walmart or Starbucks.

As we turn off towards the beach in Tulum, we enter a narrow road where my taxi driver swerves this way to avoid a bicyclist, veers that way to make way for an oncoming car, slows to a crawl to pass over enormous speed bumps, and generally drives much faster than I would expect for such an intimate setting.

At last we pull through giant wooden doors into La Luna Cabanas, we roll past walkway lights shaped like stars and moons, and come to a stop on a sandy driveway. I feel the ethereal magic of this place as I step onto the deck for registration, gaining my first glimpse of the white sand beach beyond the well-manicured gardens, and breathing in oxygen-rich ocean air. *Heaven.*

The hotel manager escorts me to my cabana—Casa Blanca—which is painted a bright teal and features an inviting hammock swaying over its wooden deck. Inside is a king-sized bed with mosquito netting draped all around, and a fanciful mosaic depiction of a dancing woman set into the stucco of the shower. After he leaves, I have a moment to catch my breath and realize: I am on vacation in a foreign country all by myself. It feels different and exciting.

Now what? I wonder. I decide it is time for a snack and a relaxing margarita, so I pick up my journal and my copy of *The Gifts of Imperfection* which I have been reading all day as I traveled, and head to the hotel bar. I sit at a table on the wooden veranda, overlooking the spectacular white sandy beach, and alternate between reading and gazing out at the vista, until it is dark. The hotel manager informs me there is a fun bar down the beach that I could walk to, or I could take a taxi downtown. There are only 10 units in this quiet resort, and there is no night life to speak of; but I did not come for a wild time. I've had plenty of that type of experience. I am here to breathe, and think, and connect with ancient wisdom in this spellbound terra firma.

By sundown, I have had a number of margaritas that have made me warm and blissfully relaxed. I decide to stroll down the beach and simply experience the breath of the ocean in my lungs, and the surging of saline waters at my heels.

Following this decadent walk are mysteries that shall remain the secret of La Luna.

ભ

The next morning I rise at the crack of dawn to journey to Chitzen Itza and Coba with my pre-arranged tour guide Martin Chi. His name is fascinating to me, and he explains he is half Chinese, half Mayan. Martin knows many places he can take me in his taxi, and I am excited for the adventure. It takes us roughly 2 hours to arrive at Chitzen Itza, during which time I sleep; I had too many margaritas the night before and am nursing a hangover.

What strikes me immediately about Chitzen Itza is the overwhelming experience of POWER. Imagining the pyramid in its full glory, ascending to the sky with 365 steps, roaring red against a blue sky—fear would be stricken into the heart of any trespasser or unfortunate sent to be sacrificed to the gods.

One might be tempted to attribute ignorance to the hedonistic ways of the Toltec-Aztec civilization that dwelled on these sacred grounds: but nothing could be farther from the truth. In fact, these ancient people had an amazing wealth of knowledge about their world, and everything they built and ritual they performed had intrinsic meaning. Simply the placement and architecture of their sacred pyramid is proof: built to reveal a slithering snake at precisely 3pm on the Spring and Fall Equinoxes, and positioned to align sunlight through windows at the top of the temple upon sunrise of the Summer and Winter Solstices. The accomplishments of these warrior-wisemen over 5,000 years ago is intriguing and beguiling.

For my personal journey, what occurs to me is how small I am. I am the tiniest drop in the largest ocean of time; I am a fraction of a fraction of a drop. And yet, I am large because I have been given the opportunity to continue the chain of LIFE like my ancestors before me. I am reinstituting the ancient ways by practicing Shamanism; I am reconnecting with this Earth, its plants and animals, and its spiritual energy. I realize that my journey of healing has included walking away from mainstream society, away from television and media and business and politics. I have walked away from distraction and towards connection with the world in which I live and breathe; and it has brought me peace and happiness and centeredness.

❧

After Chitzen Itza, Martin takes me to a cenote to swim. All over this southern peninsula of Mexico are underground pools of fresh water, called cenotes, which are surrounded by the rocks of the earth. In this particular cenote, I can see the roots of trees at the ground's surface as they weave and wind their way down 30 feet into the earth where they meet the waters below. I float on my back in these cool waters, gazing at the tree roots and up through the circular hole in the earth where sky expands high above. I imagine my own roots extending deep into the earth's surface, stabilizing me against life's summersaults. I reach out energetically to these tubular roots, to the life force of these trees who have managed to survive by sending tiny tendrils deeper and deeper. I pray to these roots, trees, and cool cenote waters: *Please heal me.*

❧

Our last stop for the day is Coba, a collection of monuments and pyramid nestled in the jungle. I wander dirt pathways for miles, observing trees and landscape and the worship of mankind. It is getting late, and I hustle to the pyramid so that I can climb before the sun sets and the monument closes. At the base of the pyramid, the climb is daunting, but I start putting one foot in front of the other, hands reaching forward to brace myself on higher and higher steps. The steps are not quite a foot length but higher than normal, requiring an effort to push my body up, and up, and up each step. I can only focus on one step at a time. As I get higher, I attempt to turn around, anxious to get a preview of the vista, but I become disoriented and immediately return to face the climb. My focus simply has to stay on the step I am climbing, and perhaps one or two higher. There are no shortcuts. There is no elevator. There is only the step-by-step climb up. I pause every few minutes to catch my breath, and then continue climbing.

Finally, I reach the top and am amazed at the 360 degree view, high above the jungle, that the pyramid affords me. So close to the sky. So close to God. I understand why the Mayans built this pyramid. It took them closer to God, and it taught a lesson along the way.

Not only does the pyramid teach that you have to climb each and every step to get to the top. It teaches that you can enjoy the climb or agonize over it.

At the end of the day, I retire to my cabana where I write in my journal about this amazing experience. Soon the sky is filled with sparkling stars, and I nestle into my hammock to admire them as they twinkle. I am so grateful for the darkness in Tulum, for the lack of development and civilization, because it means I can see millions of stars in the sky which feels like a luxury to me. I gaze at them for hours, soaking in this experience so I can dream of it when I return home to the land of artificial light.

Finally, I am too weary to stay awake any longer. I retreat into my cabana where I prepare for bed. As I am brushing my teeth, I catch a new glow about me in the mirror and I look closer. Something has shifted...I recognize this state of being faintly from my memory.

I am happy. I am in love.

I gaze at my reflection long and deep, connecting deep inside myself and reveling in the love that overflows through my eyes.

I see you sweet soul.
I see you are filled with love and compassion and understanding.
I see you as the world sees you.
It is beautiful.

When I finish gazing, I journal about this experience and I ask Spirit:

"How can I be this authentic self in my daily life?"

Spirit answers:

"Gazing at yourself will help remind you that you have everything you need and that you are love.
Only your own wisdom can lead you to self-love. Trust yourself and your process.
Be patient. Deep wounds take time to heal."

ॐ

On my journey back home, I realize that this trip has been about learning how happy and content I can be without romantic love. I went to an extremely romantic place, where couples go for honeymoons, and I went by myself. It was a brave thing to do, and it was enlightening and liberating. I realize that this experience has shown me the essence of my happiness by making me walk the path myself. No one can walk it for me. I can't imagine it instead of walking it for myself. There is only the pyramid, and the slow climb of one step after another. I climbed my personal pyramid this weekend and I saw the vista of my own love and happiness spread before me on an endless ocean.

I know now what my journey meant on the evening before I departed for Tulum. It meant I must soar like the eagle so that I can see the fabric of my life from a higher perspective. Up high, looking down and back and across, I can see how I have been on a path my whole life. I can see that I instinctively knew what I needed to do to move forward to my authentic self. Leaving my ex-husband was fighting for my soul to have peace and quiet, time and space, to learn and grow and heal. I see that I do not run from my shadows, but dive in shining whatever light I can find. I see that I can honor my struggle and also witness how when my mind, body and soul are synchronized on pure love, others feel it to, and they like the way it feels. I see that I can transcend this single physical existence and remember that life flows before and after it. When I trust this truth, and free my mind, I can soar like the eagle.

ଓ

As part of working on *The Lotus and The Lily* one evening, I investigate the question: "What is keeping me from my happiness?" I ask this question of Spirit in my journal right before bed, and hope for an answer during my dreams.

Spirit answers by leading me in dream world to the familiar vintage mansion, into the parlor where I am facing an antique mirror. The familiar terror begins to rise as the white noise escalates in volume…but before it takes hold the dream abruptly ends and I wake up. *Ohhhh.* This dream represents the source of my fear that is keeping me from happiness.

The next morning I book an appointment with Gerry so I can defeat this Goliath once and for all. During our session, however, I am somewhat frustrated because for whatever reason, I am getting the clear message from Spirit that this is one problem I will have to resolve on my own without calling in the cavalry. I do glean a very important insight, however, which is that I am afraid of my bigness. This bigness is hiding in the shadows.

As I ponder this in the context of my life, I realize that as a child I learned to be afraid of being big and calling attention to myself because sometimes this caused pain to myself or those I love; more than likely, my mother.

Now that I am aware of this fear, I can transform the story around it. I consider that being big, and having a big light, is a way to help others to see better in the darkness of their own lives. My bigness can be a source of healing. So my task is to work on becoming comfortable with my bigness and power so that I can wield it appropriately.

Once I can become comfortable with my bigness, and love this aspect of myself, I can also learn to shape-shift and be small. I realize that accepting myself, and being self-aware, allows me to be empathetic and intuitive with others; it allows me to feel into the context of my interactions to size my energy, my Self, for maximum effectiveness.

Raven appears as my teacher for this new lesson, and I am grateful for her wisdom.

> *Become the Enchantress of your Life.*
> *Go into the dark and bring forth the light.*
> *With each trip into the dark, you will*
> *bring out more light and wisdom.*[62]

It's ok that not everyone loves me. I've spent my whole life trying to be loved by others. I've worn many masks to win affection and approval. I've stuffed myself down to avoid my bigness, and then criticized myself when the real me comes out and shines my big bright light.

I consider that Oprah is big and powerful. Being big is ok: with self-awareness and humility.

୧

Several nights later, as I am performing my nightly ritual of gazing at myself in the mirror for connection, I am drawn to pull the crystal that Gerry gave me out of my drawer. As I gaze in the mirror, holding my crystal in my hand, I suddenly feel an energetic trembling throughout my being, like the shaking of a washer that is spinning from off-balance to balance.

When the trembling stops, there is a new *Me* in the mirror. "Hello" I smile, and love pours out of my eyes. I am complete, and I finally understand what that means.

> *This must be soul integration! Wow!*

I draw a big heart in my journal and write:

"Welcome Home!
I'm so very happy to have you home
with me sweet one! I love you! Let's play!"

ભ

'*Trust in Love*' means trust in God, trust in the eternal love of Spirit, trust in your own self-love. Trust that your experience of life is multi-faceted and ever-changing and wonderful and vibrant. Trust that your journey will lead where you always hoped it would.

Suggestions

Live Your Life! Do not wait for circumstances to be perfect, for the love of your life to walk in the door, for everything to be just right. Live your life. Do things that interest and fascinate you. It's ok to enjoy your own life, just for you. Going on vacation alone was the most fulfilling experience of the last several years of my life. I was in a very romantic place with myself, and I enjoyed it. Would it have been wonderful to be in love in that place with a man? Of course. But this journey was about me, and loving myself, and being _for_ myself. If considering a trip like the one I took, I do recommend working up to being in a mental space where you can enjoy your own company without feeling lonely. Trust yourself and try it. You might just love the freedom it brings.

You are Your Own Healer! As a fledgling spiritual warrior, I needed lots of guidance and support to get me going on my way. I needed some quick fixes to jump start my healing; and Gerry Starnes helped me tremendously by doing the work for me of healing my original wound. But once I progressed this far in my journey, the message from Spirit was clear: It was time for me to heal myself. We are each our own Shaman. Like every other human, I walk my path alone, from birth to death. Like every other human, my experience is unique, and so are the solutions for my healing. Gathering wisdom from fellow humans is always a good idea as it adds more ideas I can try, more tools for my individual healing toolbox. But in the end, I have to put one foot in front of the other. I have to climb each step of the pyramid if I want to get to the top. No one can carry me there. There are no shortcuts.

Appreciate Yourself! You are a unique expression of divinity in human form. There is no one else like you. Appreciate what sets you apart, celebrate what makes you special.

Keep Communication Open! *The times that I have performed my daily rituals with regularity, I notice my connection with Spirit grows and I have more inner peace and joy. Checking in with Spirit through Soul Writing is an excellent wa to keep your awareness high, and stay headed in a positive direction.*

Quotes

"You have to accept yourself and love yourself just the way you are. Only by loving and accepting yourself the way you are can you truly be and express what you are. You are what you are, and that is all you are. You don't need to pretend to be something else." — Don Miguel Ruiz

"How can a consciousness that has created all of life, that expends the energy and will to consistently regulate every function of our bodies to keep us alive, that has expressed such a deep and abiding interest in us, be anything but pure love?" — Dr. Joe Dispenza [63]

"You live in a participatory Universe. Life, with all its mystery and seeming uncertainty, is nonetheless doing one thing faithfully. It is responding to you with love and intelligence." — David Owen Ritz [64]

"You can measure the impeccability of your word by your level of self-love. How much you love yourself and how you feel about yourself are directly proportionate to the quality and integrity of your word." — Don Miguel Ruiz [65]

"There is a crack in everything. That's how the light gets in." — Leonard Cohen

""Last night, as I was sleeping, I dreamt—marvelous error! — that I had a beehive here inside my heart. And the golden bees were making white combs and sweet honey from my old failures." — Antonio Machado

Shadow Dancing

From the depths of inky blackness,
my shadow births dreams
in technicolor

Knowing the path does not mean that walking the path is easy. The deepest shadows of my soul, my innermost Jenga structure, believe that love comes from outside of me; that the most fulfilling love comes from a man. I understand this deepest need and know it originated in the loving embrace of my father in the bathtub. It is very likely I have been trying to replace that lost love all these years.

The journey to self-love is not a sprint; it is a marathon. It is moment-by-moment redirection of thought. My internal Jenga tells me I need a man to be happy. My experience of the moment shows me I am generally happy alone.

At a Spirit Paths gathering one evening, I am able to identify another false belief that is deeply held. My internal Jenga says that happiness is an 'always' state; you cannot call yourself happy unless you are always happy.

I realize that I need to shift this assumption that a 'happy life' means every moment must be happy. It is natural and to be expected that where there is light, a shadow is cast. I must embrace the shadows as part of my light.

The path of transformation is unsettling and uncomfortable, but the sunshine of authenticity and becoming the person you are meant to be is worth the struggle.

CR

Regardless of my intellectual understanding that I am seeking love from outside of myself, my quest for a man continues. I forgive myself for feeling this deepest need so strongly, and for continuing to pursue its satisfaction.

I've met a man online who is witty, and clever, and intelligent, and I very much enjoy reading his poetry and talking with him on the phone. Willie says he is 50, which is older than I have ever dated before, but I decide to consider that age does not matter; that what matters is the man inside the body. After a couple of weeks of night-time talks and truly enjoying conversation, we decide to meet. He plans to come to Austin to visit me for the weekend.

When Willie arrives, I am thrown off balance because he does not seem like the same person I've imagined him to be. Paying attention to my physical response to his presence, I don't feel any kind of romantic interest in this man, but I do still hear his voice and recognize his being in his words and expression. As we visit, it's clear he is older than he has proclaimed to be. In fact, he is not 50. He is much closer to 70…he is 68.

Spirit is certainly a she-Devil—tempting me with the illusion of what I have been seeking, only to discover it is yet another window into my own longing.

As an African American man, Willie benefits from the luxury of wonderful age-defying skin compared with me who has millions of wrinkles at a mere 43. But what his skin does not disclose, his attitudes and behaviors do. He is from another era, another time too distant for me to feel a connection of the kind he desires.

Willie's age has impacted his vision, and since it is late in the day, I am certainly not going to ask him to drive home 3 hours to Dallas in the dark. That would be like sending my 68 year old mother off in a car when she has no night vision. And really, the source of my angst about Willie certainly has to do with the fact that he is old enough to be my father. Even though I have been hung up on my Daddy most of my life, I really do not want to actually date someone who could be my father. I think Spirit has gotten some mixed messages from me.

So now we have an interesting dilemma, and I have a choice: to see a vibrant man defying the gravity of his aging body, or to see a selfish old man who has deceived me. I choose the more hopeful story, and tell him we can be friends and share company. I decide that if the positions were reversed, and I was the one who was in the sunset of my existence, I would very much appreciate being seen for the colorful spirit that is me, rather than the body I struggle with daily. In addition to this revelation, I remind myself that Spirit does not make mistakes. There is some hidden lesson here for me to discover.

As we talk into the evening, in fact, I realize something astounding: this man could very well be Z in 25 years. It is most certainly what has attracted me to him, his similarity in wit and charm. So I ask Willie if there was one woman he should have married, since he tells me he has never been married. In fact, he says, there is a woman he loves very much to this day, a woman whose heart he broke over and over again in the callousness and cruelty of his youth (in this case, his early 40s).

He has remarkable clarity and ownership of his role in this situation, and I realize that this is because he has had years to consider his actions, years to regret his choices, and years to wish he had understood then what he knows now. He says his only wish for the end of his life would be that this woman would take him back so he could prove to her every day how much she means to him. So he could finally love her the way she always hoped he would.

Asleep that night, I try to make sense of this turn of events. I am sleeping turbulently, and I have dreams that wake me in the middle of the night. In one dream I am lost in a maze, trying to get to the light, but every time I see it and head that direction, a wall suddenly slams into place, diverting me down another darkened passage. I wake from this dream and silently pray to Spirit for guidance; I feel a light pressure on the comforter by my feet, followed by the swirl of the ice in my glass. Spirit is here with me. I haven't been abandoned.

> *I am filled with knowing that Spirit is teaching me.*
> *I am listening. I am dancing with Shadows.*

In the morning I realize I have been given a gift this weekend: a glimpse into what lies at the end of life. I have new awareness that every choice made along the path to our final destination is important. The end of the bridge is approaching sooner than I thought, and every moment, every encounter, every choice made along the way matters. It's the difference between fulfillment and regrets, belonging and loneliness, acceptance and readiness for the end or fear, denial, and grief. I see now that there are endless hours at the end of life to contemplate the choices made, to regret the harms caused to those we love, and to witness the effects of our selfishness or callousness.

I also see that it is very likely Z will follow the same road as Willie. It could be the end of his life before he sees, if he ever does, my *Story of Us*. Do I want to wait that long?

Awareness dawns that by continuing to hold onto love for Z, I am putting my happiness into his hands. In all likelihood, if asked outright to hold my happiness, he would decline. No one can be responsible for my happiness but me.

I realize I need to believe, to *trust,* that when conditions are sufficient there will be a manifestation. That when Spirit sees fit, when I am ready to hold my own happiness, I will be blessed with a love that answers my longing: a partner to walk with me. And, ironically, when I am ready to hold my own happiness, I won't require a partner to walk with me.

I ponder the question: what if there never materializes the relationship I've been seeking? Does that mean my life is not worth the journey? How will I choose to define my happiness, my purpose, my life as well lived? What if I am alone, like Willie, until the end of my days? Can I accept that outcome after so many years of striving for love? What does the end of my life look like in my worst nightmare? How can I transform that story into the most wondrous tale imaginable? Am I not the writer of my story, the poet of my own life?

Can I ever alter this deepest Jenga structure and finally leave behind my quest for a man?

ি

I reach out to Z one last time with an email that pours my heart into digitized words. I tell him that after 15 months I still cannot move past him, that I still love him despite all efforts to leave this love behind. I tell him of my visit with Willie, of my realizations about regrets and how Willie taught me "The heart knows what it wants." My heart knows who it wants. Every man I have dated has been compared to one man. I plead with Z, that if his heart feels love for me, please walk with me. I admit that, once again, I have deleted his number and now I cannot retrieve it, so if he feels any love for me at all, he will need to reach out to me.

A day later I decide to bake Z his favorite banana bread, laced with an abundance of dark chocolate chips. I place it in a box for Priority Mail, and enclose a printout of pages from my book, pages of my *Story of Us*.

Several days later, a text from Z appears on my phone.

> *"Hi Pinkybelle. Got ur package today.*
> *thankkkkkk youuuuu*
> *Of course it is very good.*
> *I really appreciate it. ☺"*

I ask him if he has read my book yet. He replies:

> *"Some of it. I've been wrapped up on this*
> *velvety chocolaty banana orgasma bread*
> *to do much reading."*

For the moment I am so content to be feeding this man I love, and for him to be beginning to awaken to my thoughts and the powerful feelings I have for him.

Because it is Christmas, he is spending time with his family, and days pass without hearing from him. I fully expect this retreat because of the holiday. I send him a text here and there, knowing I will not receive a response. In this silent space, I realize I am facing myself, facing my fears, facing the darkness.

◌

As the shared family Google calendar announces, the children are at my house for Christmas. Since the boys are the only children in the immediate family living close by, my mother asks if I would like to host Christmas at my new house.

I enthusiastically accept and make the plans for baking holiday breads and preparing the holiday meal. Since I have determined I want to give each person a handmade gift, made with intent especially for them, I keep extra busy in service to my family. I spend hours melting colored wax and pouring it by layers into glass vases, layering into each candle the colors that will bring harmony to each of my loved ones' lives. Bent over a hot stove, it is indeed a labor of love.

By the time Christmas morning arrives, I am relaxed and happy with a peace that descended after spending days of meditation over candles.

Special moments are shared as gifts are unwrapped and admired, hugs given and received, and gratitude and blessings expressed. When my brother and his girlfriend are exchanging endless gifts to one another, I experience the awareness that I am happy for him; it is not my time to be part of a couple. It is my time to walk independently but not alone. I have many, many friends and loved ones to walk beside me for moments of my journey. This is enough. More than enough.

When it is time for the Christmas meal, my father graciously allows me to say the blessing. It is deeply satisfying to lead my family in a moment of thankfulness. Afterwards, looking into the eyes of each member of my family, I give thanks and praise for the blessings they bring into my life. There are sparkling eyes and smiles all around. It is magical.

❨

In some aching moments, in between my own joy of the holidays with my family, and my acceptance of being single for now, I am saturated with brief bouts of loneliness. I desire connection and understanding; and I am hoping, beyond hope, for love reciprocated.

I am like a pendulum, swinging out into loneliness in one direction, and out into joy and connection in my present moment in the other direction, and then swinging back down closer and closer to my center, to peace, to contentedness.

I am reminded continually that the emotions will surface, sometimes strongly enough to saturate me, but then they will subside as my inner pendulum swings back the other direction and finds its center point.

I am reminded of yoga practice, and how this silence from Z is just another posture I must hold even though it is uncomfortable. This posture could be named uncertainty or longing.

Silence is a strange enemy. It simultaneously holds all meanings, and no meaning. It is like darkness. Out of darkness can be pulled any manner of light and creation. Just so, out of silence can be pulled any assumption or expectation or belief. To sit with silence in an awareness of not knowing, of not controlling, of not doing...this is the posture I must hold long enough to see if my discomfort dissipates entirely, or transforms into something new.

I have full awareness that I have narrowed my potentialities into two: sit with silence long enough that I can let go of the dream of Z and embrace new possibilities free of his shadow; or sit with the silence, waiting for Z to love me.

After days of this personal struggle, where I am fully facing my mirror and delving into the shadows of my own longing, my own loneliness, I hear from Z.

> *"Hey Pink. I'm sorry I've been unresponsive.*
> *My bad. But I'm on call this week and my family*
> *is in town, a bit overwhelmed at the moment."*

I can totally understand this, and relief washes over me. But then, another text comes through.

> *"I knew when I reached out originally you*
> *would 'over communicate' in true Pinky fashion.*
> *Sorry if ur feelin offended but I seriously have*

a lot goin on right now. Im tired of holiday
talking and texting. lol"

And there it is. What I have been waiting for. The truth. And it sets me free. From Z's point of view, I am just another holiday text. His interest in communicating with me is not anywhere near my level of interest in him. My love affair with Z has been blown out of proportion in my mind. I have fabricated a fantasy of my deepest desires, my sincerest wishes for my life, and cast Z in the leading role.

Like I told him in my email, I understand if he doesn't feel love for me. He can't feel love for me in his heart if God didn't put it there. I only asked him to turn around, to try again, if he felt love for me. But the truth is he doesn't. I still don't understand, and never will, why he contacted me again, knowing his own truth.

In the midst of my disappointment, I suddenly realize: I am repeating a story I told myself long ago. Clarity descends and I see that Z is my cousin, the man who broke my heart wide open and began my deepest descent into darkness. The similarities take my breath away, the most striking of which is the use of silence as a weapon. I realize that by letting go of Z, I will complete this part of my journey by learning the lesson I failed to learn the first time:

It is time to realize I have been dreaming. I must let go of the dream, wake up, and accept what is actually true with grace.

There is only one thing left to say. I text him:

"Thank you for releasing me."

My boys are especially loving tonight; they nestle on either side of me on the couch as we watch a movie together. Tonight is a blessing from Spirit to remind me that my life is overflowing with love and purpose.

❦

I decide to fire walk again. This time, I choose to believe in infinite possibility. I choose to trust myself and my experience.

I walk again, and again, and again.
I lose count of how many times I cross the fire.
I do not get burned.

The fire fills me until I am overflowing, until I am literally drunk with fire energy. I feel powerful, and blissful, and free. I feel like a child, whirling and giddy, as I dance afterwards with friends, reveling in liberation from limitation and flowing freely with pure joy.

I realize I can construct whatever dream of life makes me happy. There is no *right* answer. There is only *my* answer for *my* journey.

This is what it means to dance with Shadows
Cheek to cheek
Arms embracing the darkness
Intimately aware of the meaning in
Every step of the dance
Unafraid of the Unknown
Unattached to the Story
And yet, engaged with Life.

ॐ

Hope springs eternal, and almost as soon as I have left Z behind I am embracing a new man. At last, my deepest wishes have been answered: Andre is attentive, amorous, awesome, and authentic. He is local, has a 12yr old son, is handsome and spiritual and successful, and is divorced. And to top it off, he is a long-time client of a very good friend of mine, so I can trust that everything about him is real. My hope is at an all-time high. Finally! I have worked so hard at clearing my wounds, understanding myself, and re-engineering my internal Jenga structure into the person I was always meant to be. Now I get to receive my reward. I can finally have the love I always wanted.

I dive deep into this relationship, with absolute trust, my heart wide open. I am ready to love and be loved in return. Everything he says and does confirms that this relationship is real. After just a few days, he wants to be exclusive; he wants me to be his girlfriend. I am overjoyed.

I make love to this man: wild, passionate, and with total abandon. What no man has ever done before, he does for me: I have a full and mind-blowing orgasm while having sex with him, chills all up and down my body. Something deep inside of me shifts, some primordial instinct locks into place, and suddenly I belong to him. "Who do you belong to?" he demands as I am climaxing. "You, Andre," I reply. "You gonna do what I tell you to?" he demands as my head is spinning and my body is in ecstasy. "Yes...anything," I relinquish control. I am home, content, and deeply satisfied with the natural order; I am absolutely vulnerable in his arms. I finally have everything I always wanted. I tell him I am in love with him. And he does what no other man has done: he asks me what that word *love* means to me.

After a long while contemplating the word love, as I am using it towards Andre, and as I have used it with Z and Robb and David before him, I come up with this definition: love is an energetic vibration that stimulates my mind, my heart, and my body. While in the feeling of *in love*, I experience it as warm, glowing, and encompassing. It makes my mind go dizzy and my heart beat faster. It makes the world more ethereal and magical. It makes me feel safe, held, cared for, desired, protected. It is the intensity of the vibration, the shifting of experience to a glowing magical state of euphoria (for example, during intimacy like kissing or intercourse) that makes me want to use this word. I suppose for me, being *in love* is an energetic message that triggers primal female responses of submission to the man and desire to please him and be *his*. I can have sex without feeling in love; so the experience is beyond the physical. It's physical, emotional, and intellectual.

In thinking over all the times I've used the word love, it has been when I am in contact with a man with whom the energetic and mental connection is highly likely to lead to other forms of love when not *in intimacy* as the relationship grows, and shared moments expand to reveal greater and greater connectivity. Other types of love would include friendship to start, and this is experienced over time as conversation occurs, ideas and perspectives are shared, boundaries are observed and challenges overcome, as we dance around each other and learn the nuances of each other. In other words, feeling in love during intimacy has become a sign to me that there is depth to be pursued in that relationship. It is a sign that the Universe has brought us together for learning and growth and connectivity. With trust, I abandon myself to the experience and allow myself to dive into it without reservation, knowing that the attention I give to this new connection will yield a crop of self-understanding at the very least.

When I am in this initial awareness of being in love, I want to be held, protected, and cared for in his arms. I want to satisfy his desires and please him physically, mentally, and emotionally. I want to be his.

My feeling of in love makes me want more of the man's attention when we are not being intimate. While we are apart, I am curious about him, about what he is doing, thinking, and experiencing. I want more exposure to him and his thoughts and perceptions, more opportunities to discover who he is. I also want more opportunities to share my world with him and grow the little seed of our new relationship into a weathered oak.

At the point that our tree has roots, limbs that reach to the sky, leaves and flowers abounding, and some knots here and there for good measure, then I will be able to say "I love you" in a way that is vastly more rich and profound.

When I share this definition of love with my friend Marques, who has absolutely no need to lie to me because he is gay, he tells me this is not the experience of a man when he is first having sex with a woman. Indeed the woman feels all of these things. But the man, he is only thinking of the next position in which he can fornicate with this woman. For a man, love comes much later.

When I share this definition of love with Chrispy, he says, "That's not love you're talking about. That's sexual attraction. That's chemistry. That's infatuation. 7th grade infatuation. Love happens quietly with years of shared moments."

∞

If you have been paying attention to my patterns, you already know that things are not going to work out with Andre. But maybe you don't know that Andre actually causes a shift in perspective that leads me much, much closer to deep and abiding self-love. There are forces in life that propel you into situations painful enough that you finally decide to grow. For me, Andre is such a force.

Everything I thought A stood for is an illusion, as it turns out. In fact, A stands for adulterous. My friend John sees how wrapped up I am in Andre; and since he understands how men think, and he is looking out for me, he does some research. What he finds sends me to my knees before God once more. Andre is not divorced. He is still married. He has lied to me this whole time, right to my face, while he is inside of me. He has, incidentally, also lied to my friend for over a year about being a single father. I am furious at this deception, at having given this man power over me because of the sexual breakthrough he was able to deliver to me; at having trusted him and believed everything he said to me; at having subjugated myself to him; and at knowing, now, that I will not get any more of those fabulous orgasms.

I am *pissed*. I lash out. I do not even bother to call him, or arrange a face-to-face meeting to ask him personally about this new information. I simply fire off a text message telling him I know he is still married and to never contact me again. In my deepest Jenga structure, I already know the truth: I cannot really have love from a man. It was all a lie designed to give me false hope and then rip it away.

I grieve with deep racking sobs for hours in the tub. Why is God punishing me? What have I done wrong? Why does this keep happening to me? Why does the Universe keep torturing me with men who are unavailable? Why am I not good enough for love to blossom?

After a while of pleading, praying, and begging, a remembrance surfaces in my mind: Everything that happens to me in this life is for my own good; for the progress of my soul. I pause and consider this truth. What have I overlooked here, in this deep treachery? What good is there in this for me?

I remember something Spirit said to me: "Trust and love are earned. Be skeptical." I have not been skeptical. I have not made him earn my trust. I have just given it freely and abundantly. I have not protected myself at all. I have put my desire for love above my own self-care.

Finally calm, I look myself squarely in the mirror. Seeing the woman in front of me, I decide enough is enough.

"I will not do this to you again, Kerri" I promise myself. "I will not give away your time, your attention, your energy, or your love until it has been well earned."

And I add: "I will never date someone again without a full background check."

∞

The next morning, after Andre has angrily responded to my text and reciprocated by ending the relationship (while still denying he is married), I realize my view of life has shifted because of Andre. I can finally see that depravity, deception, hate, fear, callousness, greed, avarice—it's all real. There really are people without good intention; it's not all a matter of misunderstanding or people colliding and inadvertently hurting one another. There really are people who take advantage of others with full knowledge and intention, and who absolutely do not care about the consequences of their actions. There really are those who will say anything to get what they want, who care only about themselves and own needs—and they do so without regret or remorse.

Whatever story Andre made up in his mind about what transpired between us allows him to escape responsibility for his actions because he can still go to church on Sunday and present the image of himself as a good person to his community and family.

In the presence of this new knowledge, I see the importance of looking out for myself, of caring for myself, and of protecting myself.

I see the wisdom in waiting for men to earn my trust and love through friendship and shared experiences.

For the first time in my life, there is a *moment* where I do not want romance; I do not want a man in my life. I am enough. I am more than enough. Paying attention to my experience of romantic love, the most consistently happy I have been is when I am by myself, reading my books and doing art, spending time with my sons, writing this book, and talking to God. Every romantic relationship with a man that I have had has been filled with turmoil, control, misunderstanding, and doing everything to give the man what he wants so he will give me love. The only person who has been there through every romantic encounter, and loved me every step of the way, is that person behind my eyes: that soul that stares back at me in the mirror. *Me.*

So my journey to self-love takes a giant leap forward thanks to Andre's betrayal. The realization dawns that the only person in this world that takes care of me, that gives me love unconditionally, and that has my best interests at heart—is my soul. Others might have good intentions, it is true. And I have many good, dear friends to attest to this truth. My sons love me, it is true. My parents love me, it is true. But the only person that loves me unconditionally, every single day of my life, is the soul that animates this body, that gives me consciousness, and that remembers I began as divine expression in human form.

As Don Miguel says, each of us is the star in our own story of life. In our own story of life, we are the main character, and we have other leading roles; but the only role that truly matters is our own. The other characters change all the time as we write and rewrite the story of our lives.

I am not perfect. I feel victimized by Andre's deception; even though I know his deception was never about me. I feel disappointed that I had to slog through the full range of emotions—denial, anger, vengefulness, sadness, fear—even though I only knew him a short time. When I reflect on this, I realize that my emotional rollercoaster was not about deep emotion for Andre, it was about my experience of deception, my experience of my world changing beyond my control, my experience of my fantasy world being shattered. I had to walk every step up the pyramid of Andre's deception to process my feelings and reach the vista at the top where the true gift of this experience lies: self-understanding and intentional transformation.

My experience of Andre taught me this lesson: I am the only person who matters in my story of life. I finally understand what self-love means—it means taking care of me, first.

My journey to self-love has a new vista, a new beginning. I choose to let go of the old life, the old wishes, the old expectations because I finally see them for what they are—chains that bind me to an unfulfilled existence because deriving love from outside of yourself exposes you to the whims of the world. It's not that I will give up on the idea of a life partner; it's that I embrace the truth: I am the only person who can give me unconditional love.

⁓

A new chapter in my life is beginning. In this new story of my life, my focus, intention, and love will go to first to myself, and then my sons. Until my love has been earned by a man—over time and experience—I will not give myself fully. Perhaps I can never give myself fully to another person because to do so is to lose me; and now that I've found me, I don't want to ever lose myself again. Maybe there is a new vision of love where, when I find the right partner, I won't have to lose me to love him.

⁓

I have been thinking of Andre for weeks every time I heard *One and Only* by Adele, but now I realize, this is the song I must sing to myself.

I dare you to let me be your, your one and only Promise I'm worthy to hold in your arms
So come on and give me a chance

To prove I am the one who can walk that mile
Until the end starts

Life is in the paradoxes. I know I need to be my one and only. Yet I doubt I will stop hoping for a life partner; my deepest Jenga structure desires the warm glow of romantic connection. I know there will be disappointments on the way to finding my man. The world is full of people who are starring in their own life movie, with their own unique perspectives and agreements about how to live and love. What agreements will I choose to make with myself? Will I choose disbelief and distrust? Or will I choose to maintain faith in the essential goodness of humankind, and keep my heart open even though I have experienced the truth that this world contains deception?

Can I forgive myself for being human? Can I forgive myself for having to walk each step to the top of the pyramid, for having to feel and process each emotion on the way to self-understanding and transformation? Will there be a day that I can simply abstract the experience, see the truth (this wasn't about me, I bumped into something unpleasant) without having to fully experience all the emotion? And is this even a realistic expectation given I am human?

Can I accept my essential nature as a hummingbird? That I fully immerse in each experience, losing myself in the moment? Is there a way I can accept the gifts of my nature? That my intensity and propensity for plunging into new situations might be a good thing in that it moves things along quickly so that I get to the discovery part a lot sooner? How would I feel if I had learned the truth about this deception in six months, or a year? Can I accept my nature and allow this to be my discovery process?

Can I ever truly face my shadow and remove that last block in my Jenga structure and embrace being alone, or even love being alone?

No matter how I answer these questions from moment to moment, I choose to engage Life with my whole heart in every moment, no matter the outcome of decisions made all around me. Even if no one participates in my story, if no one shares my journey, it is still a life worth living. I see the beauty and symmetry and magic in it. I see fireflies glowing at night and dayglow hummingbirds darting in daylight, reveling in the sea of Life. I see a life graced with compassion and love and joyful expression. I see a strong resilient woman with a positive attitude and a joie de vivre. I see *me*.

ᘓ

When we are born, our heart is the first organ created. Its tiny beat is the first sign of life detectable from the sonogram.

We are born as love.

Everything life puts in our path is an attempt to return to love. To feel love in every moment,
with every person, in every living thing.
The goal of our life is to remember who we are:
We are love.

Suggestions

Apologize! Don't delay on this one. Right now...you know what you need to do, what wrong you have to right...set your soul free of it. Bare yourself with the utmost humility and vulnerability, with nothing to gain for yourself but peace of mind... and apologize. No bells and whistles necessary. A simple "I'm sorry" will do. Your apology must be given freely without expectation of personal gain.

Expect to be Tested! The most interesting thing about spiritual learning is how quickly Spirit will test you in the lesson you think you've learned. When you come to a new awareness and make an agreement with yourself to make different choices than the ones you have previously made, expect to be tested. Expect Spirit to present you opportunities to practice your new agreement.

Change Takes Time and Constant Effort! There is no magic pill for change. There is only constant relentless awareness and a determination to make different choices than the ones that come naturally to us.

Dive Into the Shadows! Although the shadows are scary because it's dark and you do not know what is lurking there, you will never be more than the sum of your woes until you face what is lurking in the inky blackness. Generally, the fear of the darkness is greater than anything you could actually find in there. Imagine you are fearful of entering a dark closet, but when you finally shine the light inside, a cute fluffy bunny is waiting? I know that seems impossible because of the judgments we cast upon ourselves for past actions. But fear of the darkness is much greater than facing what lies within it.

Practice Clear Perception! The greatest cause of my suffering was living in fantasies in my mind. Practice seeing what is truthfully, factually, right in front of you, rather than immersing yourself in a fantasy recreation of how you wish things were. When the mirror shatters between fantasy and reality, it is devastating. So save yourself the heartbreak by staying present with curiosity about reality.

Quotes

"The spiritual warrior is the master of her own attention. Choose wisely." — Kerri Hummingbird Lawnsby

"The highest reward for a person's toil is not what they get for it, but what they become by it." — John Ruskin

"Continuous effort — not strength or intelligence — is the key to unlocking our potential." — Winston Churchill

"...as long as you stay the same person, as long as your electromagnetic signature remains the same, you can't expect a new outcome. To change your life is to change your energy—to make an elemental change in your mind and emotions. If you want a new outcome, you will have to break the habit of being yourself, and reinvent a new self." —Dr Joe Dispenza [66]

"Life is not about answers. It is about learning to live in the middle of complete uncertainty, and doing so gracefully." — Swami Chetanananda

"What's really transformative is our willingness to keep going, our openness to possibility, our patience, our effort, our humor, our growing self-knowledge, and the strength that we gain as we keep going. — Sharon Salzberg [67]

"A man sooner or later discovers that he is the master-gardener of his soul, the director of his life."
— James Allen

"Enlightenment is not a peak experience. It's a permanent shift in paradigm that deepens day by day."
— Shinzen Young

"None but ourselves can free our minds." — Bob Marley

"Nothing others do is because of you. What others say and do is a projection of their own reality, their own dream. When you are immune to the opinions and actions of others, you won't be the victim of needless suffering." — Don Miguel Ruiz

Light Illuminates Shadows

"The test of how far your wisdom has matured lies in the strategic skill with which you can keep yourself from doing things that you like to do but that would cause long-term harm, and the skill with which you can talk yourself into doing things that you don't like but that would lead to long-term well-being and happiness. In other words, mature wisdom requires a mature ego."
— *Thanissaro Bhikkhu*[68]

The last chapter was the intended finale for this memoir, but Spirit has other plans. The spiral of my pattern circles outwards and upwards and it has only been two weeks since Andre and already I am dating a new man, Christian.

His words speak to me of integrity, of radical honesty, of love and trust given freely up front because the risk is simply a broken heart. He speaks of great rewards for trust—love shared between two people. I am a cobra, fierce and lunging with venomous fangs until he speaks. Then I am dizzily swaying to the love poems of the snake charmer. He deftly defangs me.

ॐ

It is going well with Christian (it has only been one date and a couple of phone calls), except for a single word that has been shouting inside my head. In fact, the voice uttering this word has been getting louder each time I have engaged in intimacy with a new man. I have shushed that voice inside my head, I have cringed from that word, I have denied its existence, I have blatantly lied without concern for anyone but myself and my own selfish needs to feel intimacy and embrace in the arms of a man.

Herpes

ॐ

I am 22, a graduate of the esteemed Smith College in Northampton, Massachusetts, and I have not been able to secure a job in a year despite my Ivy League credentials. I take a leap of faith on a whim and fly to Silicon Valley in search of work. Within three weeks, I am hired as a technical writer, blending my skills in writing with the understanding of computers that I have gained from studying computer science as a minor in college, at the insistence of my father. Now I am thanking him for his wisdom, which felt like torture during all those hours of struggling with computer programming assignments.

My mother drives across country with me, all of my worldly belongings stuffed into our family minivan. When we arrive at the flat in San Francisco where I am renting a room, we are greeted at the door by Peter. His eyes light up when he sees me, and without any shyness whatsoever, he allows his gaze to travel the length of my figure as his smile widens. My mother is not pleased with this turn of events because she sees pending disaster.

I move into my room in this four bedroom flat where my landlord is hardly ever present, and the other rooms are occupied by Peter, myself, and Mai who is from the Philippines.

ભ

It is the first time I have ever been on my own without family close by, without friends to visit, without security of any kind. I am intensely lonely. I spend my time outside of work running from the flat in Presidio Heights all the way down to Fisherman's Wharf and back up millions of steps where I collapse exhausted.

I am trying to make friends at work, but there is only one young woman my age at work and she is uncomfortable around me. I see the way her eyes dart nervously when I am around her boyfriend, as if I am going to steal him away right under her nose. I spend hours talking with friends on the phone, friends who are 1500 miles away. I explore the city by myself, trying my hand at this new independence. However, I simply ache with loneliness.

When Peter offers to show me around town, I gladly accept. I am so eager for companionship. I fall right into the trap my mother saw coming from miles away. I end up sleeping with Peter. And, as it turns out, he is also sleeping with Mai, our other roommate. I can hear them when they do it. It makes me insane.

What is worse is that within a few weeks I am noticing something is wrong with me. I have pain in my genitals; it burns and itches. After days it is only getting worse. Finally, it is raging so horrendously in my body that I have to go to the hospital because I cannot relieve myself, I cannot urinate, and my belly is swelling bigger and bigger.

At the hospital they insert a catheter inside my urethra and release the urine. They investigate my swollen genitals and they give me the news: I have herpes. I wear a catheter and a urine bag on my leg for two weeks while I heal from the initial onslaught. After they remove the urine bag, I have to press cold wet toilet paper against my genitals in order to release the urine when I go to the bathroom. I have to visit the bathroom often because it always feels like I have to pee.

I am so angry at Peter for giving me this painful consequence of unprotected sex. I scream and yell at him and Mai, showing them my urine bag and the catheter I have to wear around. They are both shocked and checking themselves for signs of the virus. They simply did not know that somewhere along the line they had contracted it from some other random sexual encounter.

I meet my husband-to-be, Tom, during the time of this fiasco. He is a bright shining light in the midst of a lot of pain and suffering. At first I am pretending that I am perfect and everything is well in my world as we sit down for pizza at our first date. But I have to go to the bathroom, and it takes a very long time to coax my injured urethra to urinate. I'm in there an extremely long time. I make it through the evening with my date wondering what is up with me, but in the days very shortly after that the truth simply must come out. I tell him what has happened to me, and that I am moving out of my rental and down to the peninsula.

A miracle happens: he chooses me despite my imperfection. He knows I have herpes and he takes the risk he will catch it from me because he feels so strongly for me. He helps me move out of the flat, and start fresh.

I am living in my integrity. Honest, open, and caring of others. And I am accepted and loved and safe. Tom brings order to my chaos.

∝

As my marriage is ending, and I am on my own and beginning to date, I confess my herpes to a man I am interested in dating and he says "Thanks for telling me, but no thanks." All the old feelings of betrayal and unworthiness return from my youth and I feel undesirable. I try again with the next date and receive the same result.

I begin to hide the truth because I can't face this rejection time and time again. I choose to trust the medicine I take to prevent the spread of the disease. I choose to take my chances, and his, each time I have sex with a man and do not tell him the risks he is taking.

(Of course, I am taking an incredible risk with my body because I am having unprotected sex with the large majority of these men. And I do not ask for their sexual history; I do not concern myself with protecting my body from whatever diseases they might have.)

I lie to every single man I date including Christian. The word is at the tip of my tongue, it is shouting in my brain along with another voice that says "Stop hurting people, Kerri."

I fail. I am silent. I do not speak the word that is crushing me. And I engage in intimacy with this man. I know it is wrong, and I do it nonetheless. I put my own need for intimacy and affection above his life, his health.

After a week of holding back this truth, of witnessing this man and all he has to offer, I realize I cannot start a relationship with this lie between us. I realize I have to shine the light into this shadow and expose it and deal with it. My soul demands that I take action, that I speak words to bring myself into integrity before myself and before God.

I call Christian and before I let fear grip my tongue I set the words free into the phone and they are met with his silence. It is unbearable. I have wronged this man with untruth. And what is more, he could suffer physically from exposure to this virus because he tells me he has an autoimmune deficiency. My heart plummets into despair. All the lies I have told myself to justify my behavior crumble with this truth: my actions could actually cause harm to another person. It is not lost on me that I have lacked integrity much the same way Andre did.

I suddenly realize how unworthy I am of love, of relationship; I am hearing his words, his wounding, and his fallen perception of me, of the person he thought I was, the person I presented to be. I cannot bear looking into this reflection of myself, and I tell him goodbye.

A half hour later he is texting me that he is hurt I would give up so quickly on him, that I clearly do not care about him. This is not at all what I am feeling; I am feeling my own lack of worth, it is not about his worth at all.

With his continued communication, I see a doorway to possible healing, and I step through it. I drive three hours to see him outside of Dallas. As I am driving, I am sobbing and praying to God. I know that I am only going on this journey to face myself, to face the consequences of my actions. I do not hope for anything more.

As I am waiting in the hotel lobby for him to arrive, I am feeling immersed in guilt and remorse and preparing myself to face the truth of the consequences of my actions. Suddenly, my phone rings and it is Robb. He says his angels told him I need him; he tells me that he can feel I am in pain and wants to be there to help. This is such sweetness, such comfort in a moment of despair, but it is also torture because I realize I must also confess myself to Robb, to this sweet man who has reached out as a friend to me. I am not ready to face him in this moment; I am not ready to be unveiled in front of Robb; I am not ready to be knocked off my pedestal. I know this is Spirit lighting the path I must follow next, and I cringe at the task ahead. Even still, hearing Robb's voice nourishes me deeply, and I am grateful for his call.

Christian wants to take me to drink wine and eat appetizers while we discuss our situation. I am not sure I can do this without crying, but I pull myself together, put on some makeup to cover up my tear stained face, and bring my awareness to the fact that I am here for this man's healing, not to share my own pain and grieving at my lack of integrity.

Much to my surprise, we actually discuss all the matters between us while we sip full bodied cabernet and eat a delectable selection of cheeses. I am able to calmly apologize to him face to face, to explain why I was not truthful, and to look into his eyes and see the reflection of my actions—all without crying profusely or creating drama. And he forgives me. He spends the night and chooses, of his own accord, to expose himself to the virus by sleeping with me. I am relieved, and feel safe and loved in his arms. A certain measure of satisfaction arises within me. I have won my own integrity back. My word is now impeccable.

Not only that, but I have been able to communicate clearly about a difficult subject with someone who is unhappy with my actions. I have been able to calmly explain my behavior from my authentic heart, without drama, without running away, without hiding, and without lashing out. Essentially, I've behaved like an adult, and that feels solid and grounded.

○岛

I am emotionally exhausted and it has only been a month and a half since the New Year began. In a little over a month I have been immersed in two extremely intense relationships with men, each of which has drained me of resources, pushed me to my edges, and left me feeling weak and dilapidated. I am thirsty in the desert, and although Christian says he wants to continue, he has withdrawn from our former level of communication leaving me doubtful.

I have a weekend free from the children facing me, and no clear plans. I know a change is needed. I need to break my habits, change my focus, and recharge my batteries. I need to save myself. Now.

After I type a plea to my friends on Facebook to help me find productive things to do for the upcoming weekend, Spirit sends me the sign I have been seeking: a weekend retreat with Vanessa Stone a short way from home.

I heard Vanessa speak during an interview with HeatherAsh Amara and was impressed with her background as a humanitarian leader. I remember how I was drawn to the love and wisdom that emanates from her when she speaks, and determine I must go on this retreat.

I have never been on a retreat before, and this one includes lots of silent meditation. While I spend a lot of time in silence at home, never turning on the television and rarely music, I am unsure of what it will be like to spend three days in a great deal of silence.

Just after dusk I arrive at the retreat center which is a lovely expansive home and community center designed by an artist. It is just past time for dinner and thirty-some-odd people are milling about washing plates, tinkering in the kitchen, gathering around a fire pit, and visiting. It is clear that many of these people know each other, and quite well. I am an outsider, but I feel welcome nonetheless. While I weave my way through women and men dressed in comfortable yoga-esque attire, I notice the walls of the home are curvaceous and organic and covered in off-white stucco. It feels reminiscent of a cave, and secret nooks reveal themselves as I wander. Making myself as small as possible to blend into this new crowd, I wait for a sign of what to do next.

People begin wandering out the back of the home and up a gracefully spiraling stairway to a room above. I follow. As I ascend the slate-covered steps, I appreciate the labor of love it took to embed hundreds of smooth oval river rocks into the façade of each step. The stairway is a masterpiece as it unfolds step by step.

At the top of the steps is a large community room where candle light flickers all around. Bouquets of flowers adorn the front of the room where Vanessa sits lotus-style in meditation. I carefully step around people seated on the floor in quiet meditation, and find a spot that is open.

I sit and close my eyes and breathe. A small eternity passes while I listen to my breath, and the breath of all those in the room. And then

Vanessa begins to speak in a soft assured tone, leading us into a guided meditation to ground us to the earth, to this moment, to our own humanity. It is the beginning of a weekend of contemplation.

When we close the sitting for the evening, and wander outside, I notice there are millions of stars in the sky. I can see them because the sky is intensely black. For a while I sit under those stars, admiring the precious gift of darkness, until finally I am too cold in this early February Texas night, and I retire to my bed.

Our task this evening is to write what our heart center feels like at this moment, and to contemplate what living for our soul would mean to us.

I visualize my heart center. It feels like an aged apple tree in winter. Limbs have been pruned, bark stripped away in many places, and it is vulnerable and regenerating from the core. My heart bears no fruit right now. In my youth, it bore many bountiful seasons of apples; seemingly effortlessly the limbs of my heart drooped and sagged with apples-a-plenty. I realize that now, I accept that there may be fewer harvests from my apple tree, from my heart's core. I want my apples to taste delicious. The quality of the apples is more important now than the quantity. As long as my apple tree can still, someday, bear fruit…

To complete the second missive, I contemplate living for my soul. At this moment, living for my soul would mean allowing myself to pursue experiences that give me joy—without judgment or *should* or over analysis. It would mean allowing myself to travel simply because it nourishes my need for new experiences in the world. It would mean loving freely simply because it feels good to share love. It would mean arriving at a place where I can accept what this moment has to offer. Out of this clarity comes my current truth.

I am angry.
I am angry that how I am naturally is somehow wrong and needs to change.
I am angry that how I am naturally means I have a label called BPD.

This new awareness feels heavy; but it also feels extremely authentic. I spend so much time flitting about in fantasy land, playing with butterflies and hummingbirds in the land of *I Wish*, that to hear the truth uttered from my quiet, exhausted soul is somehow refreshing. With a sense of accomplishment, I tuck myself into bed for the night.

Sometime near the dawn I wake with a dream fresh in my mind, fresh enough to capture it in my journal.

> *In my heart is a little girl*
> *dejected that she has done something wrong*
> *that displeases me. That her very nature and*
> *impulses displease me.*
> *But she does not displease me.*
> *She is lovely. She is full of light and joy.*
> *She is creative and spontaneous.*
> *She is open hearted and loving.*
> *She is only doing what Daddy taught her.*
> *Because she likes the feeling of love and protection and acceptance that comes*
> *when she pleases a man.*
> *But maybe she just doesn't know other ways to get those feelings.*

When we meet at the morning meditation, Vanessa tasks each of us with venturing into the land and finding or creating a representation of our own hearts from whatever natural elements we find. In silence we proceed from meditation to perform this introspective assignment, each following our own paths. I wander down by Jacob's Well and sit on the rock overlooking the water. My heart. What does my heart look like?

As I ponder this question, I realize my heart is heavy and tired. I have been writing this memoir, looking deeply at my life and my patterns, and delving into my diagnosis of borderline personality disorder. I am ruled by my BPD patterns. All the drama created in my romantic relationships can be blamed almost exclusively on these seemingly unrelenting tendencies. No matter how much I intellectually understand my patterns, and why they keep occurring, I feel powerless to break free. My heart is tired of being inspected, picked apart, and analyzed endlessly.

I notice this branch on the ground nearby. It has two arms: one arm is straight and strong, and the other is twisted and gnarled with strips of wood separating and joining, creating gaps and the appearance of wildness. I start peeling the bark away from the branch; it pulls away in narrow strips. It becomes a meditation. Before long, I have a pile of what looks like tree hair. The straight and strong branch is clean and presentable; the wild branch is still wild…it cannot be tamed. I realize that the wild branch is my BPD. I am angry at this wild branch. Why is it tormenting me? Why can't it be straight and strong and true like the other branch? Why does it have to come apart and twist and be unruly?

I am also angry at the pile of tree hair on the ground. I am angry because that is what I have been doing to myself: peeling away at myself, critiquing and disassembling and picking at the scabs of my imperfection.

When I show my heart to Vanessa later, I ask her if I will ever be free of this wild branch, of this BPD? Because I desperately want to be free of it. It is making me miserable. It is ruining every chance at a relationship. It is exhausting.

Vanessa speaks and opens a new door for me to walk through. "This branch," she says, pointing at the wild one, "This branch is a gift. You have to learn what gift it gives you. But you can't learn that gift if you are letting it drive your life, and you can't learn that gift if you are denying it has a gift to give you. This branch is just in the wrong place. Put it in the right place and you will find balance."

I confess the man rampage I have been on for all of my life, but especially the last several years. I confess all the times I've had sex with strangers, all the bottles of wine I've consumed alone in my home, and the powerlessness I feel to stop.

"100 days of celibacy," Vanessa declares. "You will not find the deep love you seek in the human marketplace. Let God make love to you. Give God a chance."

I try to bargain down to 30 days. Vanessa is amused. "What's so hard about 100?" I don't think she understands my level of man addiction.

Three burials are what I am tasked to perform. Three things I am willing to give up.

Dear God

I offer you:
My obsessive pursuit of a romantic and sexual relationship with a man.
100 days of celibacy from sexual experiences.
My borderline personality disorder so you can use these gifts in service to the world.

I spend the afternoon in intention on the land, burying pieces of peeled bark from my heart, marking the graves of my intentions with stones found in the dirt, and meditating to my drum until I lose all sense of time. The stone I dig up to place over my BPD burial is in the shape of a heart; this feels deeply appropriate.

I release my intentions in a meditative drum state to the land, to God, to Spirit, to the Universe. The dinner bell rings. I rise from the last burial feeling new possibilities in the air. This evening, determined to discover the gifts of my borderline, I write a plea:

"Dear Borderline
How can you stay in my life without hurting me?
What roles can you take in my life that will serve
to make my life fuller and more connected?"

I pause for the response, and it comes swiftly.

"I can provide willingness to take risks.
I can provide unchained perception and perspectives.
I can provide intense emotion and deep connection.
I can provide empathy towards others' experiences.
I can provide impulsiveness and spontaneity.
I can provide boundless love for the world and others.
I can provide the highest joy."

I leave the retreat with Vanessa refreshed, and ready for new possibilities.

ﾟ

I visualize the 100 days of celibacy as a pyramid with 100 steps. I must stay on each step a full day. If I feel discomfort, I must simply witness the feeling and let it pass.

When I tell Christian of my new purpose of 100 days of celibacy, he disappears completely. He does not respond to texts or phone calls. It is clear what the meaning of our relationship has been to him. I let him drop away.

After 6 days climbing the pyramid, David contacts me because he says he misses me. I invite him to come over so that I may confess to him that I have lied about the herpes. I am working my way through the list of men with whom I have had sex, even up to a year and a half ago, and telling them the truth. With each call, I am regaining my integrity and closing a chapter. Surprisingly, each man understands about the falsehood, and none of them have caught it from me which offers a welcome relief for my guilt.

It is very hard to tell David because of how I feel about him. I do not want to disappoint him. I am ashamed, and hide my face. I almost cannot make the words come out.

He tells me to sit beside him, and I bury my head on his chest and confess. There is a pause while he takes this information into his being; then he strokes my hair and says "I love you anyway." We make love and I fall off Step 6.

The next day, I am judging myself for falling off the step, and wondering what to do about it. Should I start over again? But the more I consider the situation I realize that my climb up the 100 steps of this pyramid is the same as meditating. The practice of meditation is not to forcefully prevent thought with the notion that occurrence of thought equals failure to meditate. The practice is to observe without passing judgment or holding onto the thoughts that arise during meditation.

Similarly, my practice and intention of celibacy is to bear witness to myself in reaction to this intention, in immersion with this intention; not to sit in judgment when things do not evolve as I intended. I am bearing witness, observing reaction/behavior, and renewing intention afresh. I witness in myself a deep need for love from a man. To hear David tell me he loves me fills me up; he makes me feel whole.

⍟

Continuing my herpes confessions, it is now down to a difficult conversation: Andre. I debate whether it is better to *not* confess and let sleeping dogs lie, or confess and take my chances that the reception will not be welcome. I decide that my integrity is more important than the fear of facing a negative reception. I call him.

Andre surprisingly understands as well, and says he will simply go to get tested. I have a pang of regret that what seemed so wonderful at first was ruined by the crazy in my mind caused by my BPD. After we hang up, I can't stop thinking about it. What if? I text him that I'm sorry I reacted the way I did, that I was not able to wait to ask him in person about his marital status, that I leapt to conclusions and lashed out. He calls me back, and during the course of the conversation essentially augments my already torturing judge by telling me it's too bad I sabotaged the relationship but it's too late to go back. And yet, he has not really ever come out and said he is not married. The need for certainty, to know if I was **wrong**, is pervasive and unrelenting.

The next day I am browsing Facebook and on a lark I visit his wife's page. There is a new photo of the two of them on her profile, smiling and enjoying a meal together, holding hands; and on her finger is her wedding ring.

Liar!

Anger boils inside of me and joins with jealousy in a deadly concoction. I am enraged that he would make me feel that I am wrong, that it is my fault things did not work out. That he would lie to my face again, even though there is no reason to lie. I am so livid I do not know what to do with myself.

I screen capture the picture on her page and send it to him in a message on Facebook.

*"You are a fucking liar! Why in the world would you lie about this and make
it seem like it's my fault we broke up when you are MARRIED?
At least you gave me great material for my book!"*

I am incensed. And even this hurled dagger does not make me feel
better.

Bad turns to worse: the idea that I will be writing about him in my
book ignites anger in Andre. He calls. I see his number and do not
answer, but when I listen to his message I hear his verbal threat:

*"If you cause problems for my family or my business or my reputation, YOU
WILL PAY, and it doesn't matter who you know."*

I am further enraged that he would threaten me, and I text him back:

*"God will take care of you Andre. That is not my job.
Your name will not appear in my book, but the story of my encounter with
you, and the lessons I have learned about the darker side of human nature
will.
I hope you will not choose to involve any other women in your deranged
world."*

I am standing in a raging fire deliberately. Do I want to get burned?

&

When I tell Chrispy of the recent events, he is concerned with the
Andre situation. "7 out of 10 women are beaten or raped or killed,
Kerri. That is not a good statistic for you," Chrispy warns.

Awareness dawns on me that I have kept company with a man who
would kill to protect his fabricated construction of a life, his castle
made of sand. I have been vulnerable with a man who wears the
mask of a saint, but underneath is a devil.

What compels me to prod a tiger with a stick when there is no barrier
between me and him? Do I believe I am bullet proof? Where is all this
rage coming from? Why can't I let this go?
I hardly know this man. He doesn't even matter in my world.

&

Wise advice comes my way that before I attempt to publish a book, I should read other authors who have previously published in the same genre or topic. There is a very short list of books published by authors about borderline personality disorder.

I start reading *The Buddha and the Borderline* by Kiera Van Gelder. Instantly as I read, I am seeing similarities in our thinking and patterns, and find myself saying *"yes!"* out loud or bursting out crying to hear that someone else has felt the same way as me.

"In my life, relationships are like rubber bands. They stretch and snap back so many times, but eventually something breaks and there's no way to repair the damage." –Kiera Van Gelder

So many times I have felt this way, except I have felt that I am the rubber band, stretching, stretching, stretching and then *snap*! Once I snap, the other person is aware that my cool exterior is not what is really happening under the surface, and the cat is out of the bag. With Tom, he was able to keep coming back after each snap; it was me who eventually was tired of stretching, stretching, stretching.

She talks about her diagnosis, and coming to terms with it:

"There's no question that the diagnosis fits. I have all the symptoms: I have chronic feelings of emptiness and an unstable sense of self. I'm suicidal and self-harming, and I frantically avoid abandonment and rejection no matter what the cost. My relationships are stormy and intense, and my perceptions can shift between black and white at the drop of a hat."
–Kiera Van Gelder

Ever since I was given the diagnosis by my therapist, I saw the truth in it, and yet I hated it. Seeing the list of 'qualifications' for a BPD diagnosis is like looking into a mirror and seeing all of your faults; it is hard to feel anything other than bad about yourself.

One afternoon, while waiting for my car to be serviced, I eat lunch at a nearby Mexican restaurant and drink a margarita while reading *The Buddha and the Borderline*. Feeling so connected and validated by reading this book, it almost feels like I have permission for the thoughts that course through my brain, and the feelings that rampage my heart. When my car is ready, I stop by my mother's house to drop off soccer bags for the boys (since it is Tom's weekend and there are games). While I am there, I open up to my mother about how I feel about reading Kiera's book, and about realizations I have been making.

The reception is not warm. In fact, it's hostile. I try to remain calm and composed during the verbal storm that ensues, and at one point realize that I am ill prepared to handle the anger that is welling up inside my mother and is directed at me. I try to leave, but am accused of always leaving when my mother has something to say to me. So I stay, against my judgment.

"I've talked with every one of my friends that has a daughter, and NONE of their daughters share personal information from their lives with their mothers. I DON'T WANT TO KNOW about your life! I DON'T NEED TO KNOW ABOUT THESE THINGS!" my mother gestures wildly with her arms and her face turns red as she releases a torrent of anger and frustration at the source of her pent-up emotions—me.

I've been telling my mother a lot of things from my journey, including falling off Step 6, and it has obviously been too much information.

I know I share more information than many people are comfortable with. My friends know I share more information than is standard among our peers; but for them, it is a source of amusement. My mother is not amused.

"I'm sorry mother," I say. "I know I share too much information. No boundaries. Sorry. You got the borderline personality daughter." It's a feeble apology, one that asks her to see me as a victim of my disorder.

This enrages her even more. She continues her onslaught. "This book is fine for you to write, but you can't show it to anyone. This will destroy our family!" The real source of this outburst revealed: What will everyone think when they know the truth about me? About my affair with my cousin? About my sexual promiscuity? About my childhood abuse? And underneath it all, what will everyone think about my mother?

Once the flood gates have opened, it must all be released. I know this from history. It will all come out. There is no stopping it now.

"You are just MAKING ALL OF THIS UP!" she rages on. "I think you just do this to get attention, and so you don't have to BE RESPONSIBLE for what YOU DO!"

The torrent of repressed frustration and anger continues; the acrid energy crashes over me and through me. Intellectually, I know this is my mother purging; there are elements of truth to what she is saying, but her intent is not to hurt me. I have unconsciously been poking at her deepest regrets, fears, and shame with all of my unbridled sharing, and now her emotions are spewing out from deep within like the cap has just been flicked off a shaken soda bottle.

Although I understand the pattern, however, I cannot escape my own patterned reaction to it. At some point my inner two year old takes control with the only protective behavior she knows how to do: I start slapping my head uncontrollably.

At this, my mother starts shaking her hands above her head violently. "Oh now you're going to HIT YOURSELF?? I'm so sick of this! How about if I HELP YOU?" and she comes towards me.

The next thing I remember, my mother and I are shoving each other, slapping each other, and yelling at each other. I rip her shirt. I yell at her "This is all your fault! You did this to me! I hate you!" My Dad appears pale and confused from the back room where he's been napping. My son Tanner runs into the room, his 10 year old eyes wide and his face white.

I snap to my senses, grab my things and sprint for the door with my mother in hot pursuit yelling at me "I SHOULD CALL THE COPS ON YOU!! DON'T EVER COME BACK HERE!"

൫

I drive out of my parent's driveway and down the road before my own terror and grief finds me. I pull over in the neighborhood, sobbing. I call the only person I can call: Tom.

Sobbing, I relay to Tom what has happened. He listens, and takes in the information without compassion: just the facts, ma'am. We hang up and I drive home.

I slapped my 68 year old mother. I have never hit my mother before today. I don't remember what happened after she said she was going to help me hit myself. All I know is we were cat fighting.

The ground drops out from underneath me. I know how it works in my parents' world. They are right, I am wrong. My mother is the victim, my father is the rescuer. Now, it seems, I am the perpetrator to be hated and feared. There is no winning in their world, unless you follow their rules. There are no perspectives allowed but theirs—no other world view exists except the one agreed to and co-crafted by my mother and father. It's amazing how Spirit finally unveiled the ugliness I feel towards my mother, and she towards me. I've spent most of my life protecting her from my anger, putting her on a pedestal, and defending her from negative judgment. We've spent our lives entangled, smiling on the surface and wanting to bitch-slap each other underneath.

As I drive home in a haze, one thought comes to me over and over again: *I am tired of fighting.*

By the time I reach home I am a zombie. *I am tired of fighting.* I unlock the door and let Daddy Dawg outside in the yard. *I am tired of fighting.* My mother will blame me for everything. My father will never forgive me. *I am tired of fighting.* I don't have parents anymore. They'll never take me back now. *I am tired of fighting.* Tom thinks it's my fault too. He'll side with them. *I am tired of fighting.* I could just disappear. *I am tired of fighting.* All this work and I'm still not fixed, I still have BPD, I'm still making people upset. *I am tired of fighting.*

I run a hot bath. I dig around in the utility drawer and find the razor blades. Daddy is pacing nervously at the back door and barking. I don't want him to be trapped in the house with me. It might be days before I'm found.

The cellphone beeps a text message. It is my son Garrett, then 13, texting me. "All that stuff you're writing in your book is private, Mommy. You don't need to tell anyone your mistakes. Those are only for you to know."

I am embarrassing my family by writing this book. *I am tired of fighting.* What I have done in my life is an embarrassment. *I am tired of fighting.* My life should be kept secret. I will only embarrass my children. *I am tired of fighting.* Why go on living? *I am tired of fighting.*

I climb in the bath. I make timid marks with the razor blades. It's harder than I thought. I've never tried it. I don't think I can do it.

I make a mental check of my house and realize I have no old medicines lying about. *Damn.*

I consider making a noose, but I am no good at knots. I don't want to hang myself and live.

I burst into racking sobs. Spirit whispers.

> *These emotions will pass.*
> *What can you do to help yourself right now?*

I remember Ceci saying all sensations of emotions pass quickly. I white-knuckle it through the emotions as they course through me like tidal waves. Mere minutes feel like eternity as I sob naked in the tub.

Terri

Her name pops up in my mind and I realize it is perfect. She will know what to say to me right at this moment. I lunge for the phone and, miraculously, she answers. Through convulsive gasps I relay to Terri what has happened, and how I'm feeling, and after 40 minutes of simply being heard (and only partially understood because my sobbing makes my speech almost undecipherable), I feel ready to continue with life. The danger has passed.

To cement this decision, I make a list of reasons to live.

Reasons to Live:
-sunshine on my face
-flowers
-hugging Tanner and Garrett
-cuddling with Daddy Dawg
-laughter
-ocean waves coming to shore
-the smell of stargazer lilies
- cold sparkling water on a hot day
-being in the moment in a soccer game
-experiencing Peru
-sea turtles in Tulum
-exploring the world
-my drum

Next, I write a letter to my mother in my journal; a letter I will never send.

You are free of me mother. Even when I was in your womb, I could feel your uncertainty about bringing me into the world. Your heart was conflicted. Still your heart is conflicted. When I wear the mask of success and happiness you love me fully.
When I share the truth of me you feel shame and you push me away angrily.
I can't be in this dynamic with you any longer.
We both need to move forward.
Maybe we can't do this together.
I'm sorry I can't just tell my story in the mirror in the bathroom with the door locked like I used to as a child. I can't just 'SNAP OUT OF IT' like you yelled at me to do. When I 'snapped out of it' in the past I adopted a new mask—but stuffed everything real deep down inside me, way down into the shadows.
I did it by lying to myself and everyone around me.
I am done lying. Lying doesn't change truth. Embracing truth in the light is what creates space for change. Keeping a spotlight on my shadows keeps me from lying…keeps me from perpetrating the behaviors that only serve to hurt me in the long run.
Denying the ways I betray myself is just as harmful as judging myself for

189

them. The tightrope I am walking is to bear unrelenting witness, and give myself compassion for the struggle.
I have heard people say many times that when they embark on real personal transformation that it has strong ripple effects on the people in their worlds.
I am witnessing this truth in our lives.
I have chosen the path of 'spiritual warrior', the path of deepest personal transformation.
Perhaps it is best to limit or eliminate contact for now...until my world stabilizes.

A new chapter of my life is beginning. I have shed the marriage, and now I shed my parents; I shed the last bit of support structure that has been holding my world together....my old world. Those old structures do not apply in the new life I am creating. I have to be fearless now. I have to step out like Indiana Jones into that vast crevasse with absolute faith there will be something for me to stand upon.

I fall into bed at 6pm and sleep until the morning.

Spirit is a master at orchestrating endings and beginnings. As it happens, when I wake it is the morning of the first 13 Moons class at the Toltec Center of Intention, a women's group led by HeatherAsh Amara that is focused on embodying our feminine wisdom and power.

Still feeling otherworldly from being on the edge of leaving this existence, I manage to make it to class and find a welcome support in the company of about 40 women all seeking their own truths. During the course of the afternoon, it becomes very clear that many of us share similar demons and false beliefs that have prevented us from fully living our lives. As I craft a vision board for the next phase of my life, I decide that I can make my vision include anything that makes me happy, anything that brings me joy. I no longer need to choose directions in life simply because I think someone else might approve, or at least, won't criticize.

A new concept of life support emerges in my awareness—an interconnected web comprised of communities of spirit and healing, friends on the spiritual warrior path, my sons, and Spirit.

Later that evening, I continue reading Kiera Van Gelder's book and come upon these passages.

"As soon as someone judges, criticizes, dismisses, or ignores, the cycle of pain and reactivity ramps up, compounded by shame, remorse, and rejection. The act of validation, simply saying 'I see things from your perspective,' can help short-circuit that emotional detour. "

...

"Even if everyone in the world were to accept me and my illness and validate my pain, unless I can abide myself and be compassionate toward my own distress, I will probably always feel alone and neglected by others."
-Kiera Van Gelder

I realize that word—validation—is what I have been missing in much of my experience of growing up with my parents, and of these failed attempts at relationships. Validation is the missing link in my heart.

But now I know I need to create that link all by myself to be whole.

ভ

After class ends I drive to Houston to take over for Tom at a soccer tournament for Garrett, but it is very late by the time I arrive so we all stay at the hotel room together. I toss and turn with all the events of the last 30 hours. Sometime around 4am I wake with my mother on my mind, and I can feel anxiety and anger welling up inside my body. The unprocessed emotion is keeping me awake.

I pick up my iPhone and craft an email to her that I am sorry my sharing has caused her so much anxiety and shame, and that I hope she will seek help to deal with the emotional burdens she clearly carries around with her. I also tell her I will plan to stay away from her while I do my own life transformation, and until I am in a place where we can try again.

Later, I send an email to both of my parents and Tom with the new child care strategy which will ensure that my parents do not see me on the days I have custody of the children. There is no response to either of my communications, but I do not expect one.

When I arrive back at home after the weekend, the children are in bed and then the phone rings. It is Robb checking on me. I tell him what has been happening, and he asks me why I didn't call him.

"Because you don't pick up the phone," I tell him.

"Well I will," he says, "Use a code word...like 911 and I'll pick up. You know I love you."

Actually, I don't.

ʘ

All night I have been dreaming of vultures circling over me, and then descending and eating my stomach, ripping intestines from my belly and devouring them. When I venture outside to my porch, I see vultures circling high overhead. The vultures are roadside eating a deceased deer as I drive to take the children to school. Vultures are everywhere.

"Although their role as scavengers is often considered disgusting, [vulture] serves an extremely valuable and necessary function. It limits infections and bacteria from corpses that could otherwise spread to other animals who do not have the resistance. They serve to keep the environment clean and in balance. They prevent the spread of disease." [69]

I beckon to vulture to clean me of the emotional toxicity that has been boiling in my belly since the beginning of the year. I welcome vulture.

ʘ

Monday following the fight with my mother I am drained energetically. I set up an appointment with Gerry who performs Reiki energy work to restore my energetic balance. The smog that has permeated my head lifts while Gerry works, and I am restored with clear perception. I deepen into the thoughts I had after the fight with my mother, the thoughts of wanting to not fight anymore. I deepen into my own feelings of anger.

Betrayal is added to my emotional mix when I receive a call from the Williamson County Sheriff's Department. Apparently, my mother filed a report with them about the incident so it could 'be on the record.' Revenge is a predictable response from my mother; from that whole side of the family actually, but that is another story entirely.

I relay my version of the 'altercation' to the officer who is interviewing me for the police report. I am sure that my version is very different from my mother's version.

In fact, when I pick up my son Tanner at school that afternoon, he tells me "Nene said you are insane."

Now is my chance, I realize, to teach a valuable lesson: a lesson I have only learned since reading *The Four Agreements* by Don Miguel Ruiz.

Later that evening when my boys are eating dinner, I explain to them that every person on this planet is living a dream of their own life in which they are the star actor or actress. Since we are each living our own dreams, it is hard for any one of us to say what actually happened when an argument occurs between two people. This is because each person truly believes their version of the events happened just the way they say it did.

The only way to truly know what happened is if an impartial third person witnesses the event (or a video camera!). If a third person witnesses the event that is sympathetic to one of the people in the event, then even that perception cannot be trusted.

At least I can turn my conflict with my mother into something useful for my sons to digest. I will not hurl insults or prolong the war. I will choose to forgive, and use life's painful lessons to teach my sons and myself. I will transform what no longer serves me into something that nourishes me and my sons.

CR

When I meet Chrispy next, he astounds me with an insight I had not yet considered.

"Your folks actually believe in you, probably more than they ever have before in your life," Chrispy says. "They fully believe you're going Oprah with your book, and the whole world is going to know about the family's dirty secrets."

Wow. I had not considered that perspective. But I could see the truth. My mother's actions have all been motivated by *FEAR*. Fear of what everyone will think when they read my book. Fear of what they will think of her, of me. What the rest of my family will say. How the book will ruin everyone's lives.

Really? That assumes someone actually *reads* it.

Chrispy has another great insight: "Why do you keep going to the drive-through at McDonalds expecting Filet Mignon? The relationship with your mother does not nourish you, and has not for a long time. Why do you keep seeking nourishment in that relationship?"

My path lies in honestly seeing the relationships in my life for what they are, and in stopping my endless quest to make these relationships into my personal vision of what they should be. In almost every case, I am trying to make a relationship what it is not, failing at it, and getting frustrated and angry. I need to wake up to the true nature of the relationship and allow it to be exactly what it already is.

In the case of my mother, I have been living in this fantasy that we are a happy, bonded mother/daughter team that are really more like adult girlfriends. I have been envisioning profound life and spiritual discussions, venting about my adventures in dating, and journeying with my mother at drum circle.

The reality is that my mother has absolutely no interest in my struggles with romantic relationships, my healing of childhood wounds, or my shamanic path. My mother would like to talk about the weather while we get pedicures.

I am not going to change my mother. Trying to change my mother has made her, and me, angry. The only person I can change is myself. This means I have to give up the fantasy and embrace reality so that I can be in peaceful relationship with her. And it also means I need to fill my buckets elsewhere.

When I tell Chrispy about my recent interactions with Andre, and the fight with my mother, and the police report, Chrispy once again points out: "You are in a pattern of violence and anger. Get out of it now before something bad happens."

⅓

I lost a great deal of energy in the altercation with my mother, and although seeing Gerry made me feel better, I still am aware that I am missing energy.

In the safety of my bubble bath, I envision walking into my parents' house to the kitchen where the conflict occurred. I calmly look around for my energy, but I have no idea what it should look like. I have just heard of people reclaiming their energy during meditation, and so I am trying it out here. Spirit does not let me down. Suddenly, a little 2yr old version of me runs out from underneath the kitchen bar counter and hugs my legs, terrified. Oh wow! I hug the little girl and think that must be it, but no—there are more versions of me that materialize out of nowhere and join us. Me at 3, 6, 8, 12, 16. Soon there is a group hug going on as we reunite. I take all of these "Me" versions into myself and we leave the house.

Over the next few days, however, I keep sensing that the 4yr old me is disappearing back to my mother's house. When I go there to reclaim her, she is there by my mother's chair, concerned.

When I call Ceci about this reoccurrence, she suggests a session to explore what is going on with my 4yr old. At her office, I remember back to the first time I felt like I don't want to fight anymore—which is how I was feeling after the fight with my mother—and I am back in the apartment where my mother and I lived with mean Fred. I am in my room terrified, under the covers of the bed. My mother needs protection but I am too small to help. I am terrified because I can hear them fighting in the other room: banging sounds and my mother crying and Fred yelling. If anything happens to my mother, I am going to be stuck with mean Fred.

In this memory, I suddenly realize I had made an agreement with myself: protect my mother. This one agreement has kept me coming back time and time again to a highly in-twined relationship that has often been toxic for both of us. But she doesn't need my protection now, and hasn't needed it in a really long time. She can take care of herself. In fact, she has her knight in shining armor ready to rescue her at a moment's notice. It's not my mother that needs my protection.

It's *me* that needs my protection. I need to relinquish the fear of my 4yr old, and allow my 4yr old to embrace new love and support from my adult self as caretaker. Team Kerri activate.

That evening, I determine I need to recapitulate to release another toxic relationship—Andre. While mentally I am very much done with him, I still feel an energetic affinity I would like to eradicate while reclaiming the energy I lost by engaging with him.

While breathing in, I envision my power, energy and love returning to me as sparkly energy through the air. While breathing out, I envision his poison like black smoke pouring out and into the Earth where it can be transformed.

I relinquish the jealousy, anger, invalidation, fear, and hate, sending all that black smoke into the Earth. I let go of the need to know what really happened. I let go of the need to be right. I breathe back my soul parts given up to that experience, breathe back my joy, and breathe back my love. My mind's eye starts growing a tree: tall, wide and strong with lovely flowered vines cascading to the ground. My inner goddess plays joyfully beneath this tree with a happy 4 year old that is dancing and singing because the bad man is gone. Yay!

Spirit weaves an interesting fabric for our lives.

08

The events of the past week have raised my awareness of the entanglement that binds me to my mother. This tangled web has to be severed for me to fully live and become who I was meant to be.

As I did this time last year, I call on Kat to perform a Reiki *Cord Cutting* ceremony. Last year, I cut the cord with Tom. This year, I am prepared to cut the cord with my mother. I am ready at last to sever this bond and forage out into the world as me.

Kat is a beautiful woman with one hazel eye and one blue. I can get lost gazing between them, especially since they are so clear and pure because her energy is clean. She takes me in her capable hands and massages me to get me relaxed for this release; severing the cord with the woman who brought me into this world. It feels momentous, but I am ready.

As she begins the cord cutting, we cut through the root chakra and the red coiling light comes back into me, unbound from my mother. We cut the second chakra, and orange swirling light comes back into my creative center. When Kat puts her hands over my third chakra, however, she says it is like a vortex, pulling her inwards energetically. It makes perfect sense; entanglement with my mother has prevented me from developing a strong sense of self—the seat of my personal power, the Manipura, the solar plexus. Kat and I envision a massive golden cord connecting me to my mother from my third chakra and a giant pair of scissors... CUT! HUFF! The golden light swirls back into my Manipura, and as Kat tests its strength, she reports it is weakened, but no longer a vortex.

We finish cutting all the remaining cords, and I feel lighter, freer, and strangely there is a shift in my center of gravity—it is now coming from *my* center. I am alone in this world at last.

෪

The evening following my cord cutting, I want to celebrate my freedom. I am wishing for a nice date with someone like Christian to go have some lovely wine and hors d'oeuvres. Then it occurs to me that I can take myself out to enjoy the things I like to do. So I do! I take my NOOK and head out to a local wine bar. I pick a bold and spicy Shiraz and order melted flaming cheese with bread.

When I relay that I have taken myself on a date to my 13 Moons coach, Diana is pleased. "Great!" she says, "Anytime you notice yourself thinking of a man, notice the need that is not being filled and fill it for yourself. Homework: more dates with self."

Diana says to always remember that I was domesticated to look outside of myself for answers, for happiness. Breaking this pattern will require relentless awareness and willingness to be in discomfort while new structures are put into place in my life.

∞

A couple days later I am headed to Joshua Tree for the first course with the Four Winds Society; I am studying to be a shamanic energy healer. As I put on my vision board for 13 Moons, I intend to be the voice for those who have none; I intend to be a healer. On the way to Joshua Tree, I feel like this is a real possibility. I intend to fully enjoy this journey.

It is my maiden voyage as myself, and only myself, and I am paying attention to what that means to my spirit and body, not just my mind.

When I arrive at Joshua Tree, it means laying low, being silent, and paying attention to what is happening inside of me, rather than the hubbub of the students all around me. Soon enough, though, I make friends. When we go around and say where we are from, Jonathan, a fellow Austin-ite, notices me and chases me down later with extended hand. He's so friendly he's easy to like. Then in circle time, a woman named Lori mentions she is a Master Firewalk Instructor and I can't stop myself from clapping with giddy delight. She grins and we make instant *fire* connection! Later we make tentative plans to walk on the ceremonial fire after everyone else leaves (we do not get the chance, but it was fun planning it). It is amazing the walks of life of the students in this course who are here to learn the Illumination process: how to heal people energetically through the chakras.

I am ecstatic to be on my path at last. The next morning it feels like a week has passed already as the instructors make time bend while we learn a million things a shaman needs to know.

Most importantly, we learn about how our bodies are surrounded by a luminous energy field that many people refer to as an aura. This luminous energy field can be thought of as a liquid computer screen where 'programs' or 'viruses' get installed when traumatic things happen to us; this is the source of our repeating patterns. During this course, we will learn how to bring those viruses into the chakra where the virus dwells, and then clear them using the Illumination process.

I am very excited by this energetic healing process because, clearly, I am not a fan of spending 25 years in talk therapy which is the equivalent of wading through quicksand.

To become medicine healers, we have to transform our own 'hooks' into medicine for healing others. We are tasked with identifying our three biggest hooks. We will perform Illuminations on each other to heal these hooks in ourselves, and then the healing of these hooks becomes our medicine for our clients.

Hook 1: Validation.
I don't know how to do it myself.
I need someone to validate that I'm doing it right.
The 'A' student needs a perfect mark.
If you don't validate me, I do not exist.

Hook 2: Abandonment.
I am always choosing men that abandon me, even when there are perfectly reasonable male choices who do not abandon me. This is to prove to myself that I am not good enough.

Hook 3: Success.
I'm never successful at building a livelihood doing what I love. Every time I try to make a living from my art or creativity, it fails. So I am always stuck doing technical writing which pays the bills but does not feed my soul.

ʕ

We are tasked with building a sand painting in the desert, using burnable items from the desert to represent our current world view and the problems we are facing with our hooks. The power of a sand painting, or of the mesa I built with Vanessa Stone on retreat, is in letting the Earth, Pachamama, work the issues for you energetically. Tangibly representing your world on the surface of the earth gives you a perspective that is quite useful in contrast with going around and around about it in your mind.

In my case, I want to put a little orange stone in the middle of my painting—me—and surround it with large tough stones, like a fortress. (Later, Chrispy tells me how my fortress represents my third chakra, my Manipura or 'city of jewels'.) Above my little orange stone I draw a heart, and inside the heart I put two little stones representing Garrett and Tanner. Outside of the fortress, I place Tom and my parents. They are outside the castle walls, outside the moat, far from anywhere they can cause me harm. That is where I am today as I make my sand painting.

ʕ

Alberto Villoldo speaks to us every morning, and I simply love listening to the life stories of this man whose life has been so incredible. When I walk up to him during the break, I notice how the air shimmers around him and his entire being speaks love and compassion. I check myself to see if this is real or an illusion. But then he turns to me because he feels I have a question.

"Alberto, I have been struggling with whether to go to Peru this summer. My heart wants to go, but after being here in class just the last day I feel like maybe I should do more coursework and training before I go, maybe I should know more. What do you think?" I lay it on the line for him.

He touches my arm gently and looks right through me into my very being. "Trust your heart." He looks just past me and then returns his gaze. "Your heart has gotten you in some trouble and so you don't trust it. But trust your heart."

It is as if he pressed a button in me that said "you are allowed to be". A river of emotion gushes out of me as I walk away: thankfulness, relief, hope. It's hard to explain, but somehow Alberto gave me permission to live with just those simple words.

○

When we start working on Illuminations, I choose *Hook 1* as my first issue to be healed. I figure this issue has to do with my childhood, and the trauma I went through as a little girl that I never quite reconciled how to handle.

What I do not anticipate is the realization that I do not think the world is safe. While I am releasing the heavy hucha I hold about validation, and going deeper with the guidance of my fellow student, it suddenly becomes clear that I do not think it is safe because as I was growing up I never knew when my mother was going to be upset, or lash out in anger or frustration. I never knew when things would turn from laughing and happy to meanness and punishment. As all of this unknown emotion is surfacing, it dawns on me that I do not need to cling to my mother. In fact, clinging to my mother, not separating my identity from hers, has caused me a great deal of pain in my life.

I realize that there is another mother that is unconditional in her support, her validation, and her love: Pachamama. I am always nourished, always cared for, always guided, and always loved by Spirit and by mother Earth. The sun always comes up for a new day. There is always air to breathe, and water to drink.

My human mother was the vehicle through which I was born into this world, and of course I love her. But my real mother—the mother of us all—is the source that fashioned me out of energy, genetics, and love. Somehow, forging this bond gives me the unconditional acceptance and love I need to feel strong as I stand alone for the first time in my life.

As Alberto is talking later on, I also clearly hear the message that I chose my human mother when entering this world. I chose her for a reason, for the gifts she would require me to develop in this world. I grew up believing in past lives, so thinking along these lines is not a stretch. I ponder: what gifts have I developed as a result of living with my mother?

I have learned to be extremely sensitive energetically because of trying to sense my mother's moods.

I have learned to be diplomatic and understanding of others' situations because of my own experience of feeling like I was not heard or validated.

I have developed a great creative and imaginative mind from countless hours spent alone in my room while growing up, that now feeds me spiritually.

I have learned to listen to myself, and heal myself, from all those times in front of the bathroom mirror.

I have worked to overcome the 'learned' patterns and behaviors from childhood, and have chosen a different way of communicating with others.

I have harnessed my rebellious spirit
—born of interaction with my mother—
but I am now the rider.

ॐ

Near the end of the course in Joshua Tree, with all the various shamanic healing work and ceremonial rituals we have been performing, my experience is shifting into an entirely new world view. I perceive this shift as *fullness*.

I have never felt full before in my life. It is a really strange and wonderful feeling. During the last day of class, when feedback is solicited from the students, I raise my hand.

"Since last night's ceremony," I say, "I am not sure how, but the world is different. Everything is more luscious, more vibrant, more full of life and love."

Silently, I pray that this perception of the world remains as I reintegrate with my life at home.

ॐ

In fact, it does. Back at home following Joshua Tree, I maintain my daily rituals that I established at Joshua Tree. When I wake, I stretch and move my body with a personal yoga practice that begins with three Ohms. I move my body however it needs to move to awaken, to elongate, to move the blood through the tissues. After about an hour has passed, I move onto Kundalini Breath of Fire which moves energy from first the earth, and then the sky, into my being. Once that fire has accumulated in my belly, which I sense is a large bubble of light projecting from my abdomen, I 'feed' that light with intention into each of my chakras.

At the end of the day, I clean my chakras as I was taught at class, and then allow water to cleanse me during my nightly bubble bath. Right before bed, I open sacred space, inviting spirit to my altar, and I silently thank each of the four directions and four elements for constant support in my life.

On the days I have my children, I simply weave my rituals through the daily requirements of getting the boys up and delivered to school.

Thus, the shift I experienced in Joshua Tree continues forth at home with the steadfastness of these rituals, and I notice that I am full inside.

My fullness manifests in less physical hunger: I only eat half of a meal I would have previously finished. My fullness also means that I do not desire alcohol like before: one cocktail is sufficient for an evening, where before I would have consumed at least 2, maybe even 3. In fact, I do not desire anything above nourishment for my body because there is no need, no gaping hole, no dissatisfaction, to fill.

For once, I do not feel like I need someone else to validate me, or to make me feel happiness. I am content being in my own company.

For once, I feel like I can inject some personal discipline on some of my repeating patterns, and actually get traction towards transformation. Because I don't need anything outside of myself to feel full and complete, I can willingly let go of things that no longer serve my greater desires and life vision. And if I feel the familiar twinges of doubt and discomfort—which I have no doubt will surface along the way—I have lots of tools for releasing these blockages and moving forward. Now that I've felt fullness in my body, I can return here any time if I get lost.

୪

The rift between my mother and I is unhealed, and now is not the time to confront it in person, or to have any actual contact between us. So, for now, I trust that Pachamama will help me heal my relationship with my mother in my own heart. I build an altar for my mother in my backyard, under a lovely tree. I fill a glass box with laminated pictures of all the things my mother loves: malted milk balls, pictures of her holding my sons, the *Better Off Dead* movie, *Days of Our Lives* soap opera, mystery books by her favorite authors, Swiss Almond ice cream, and more. I light a candle for her every day or so, and say a prayer that our hearts are healed of this emotional toxicity.

୪

When I meet with Marques for dinner following my trip to Joshua Tree, he is immediately aware of the joy that emanates off of me. "Your energy has completely changed," Marques smiles, shaking his head in disbelief. "You're not the same Kerri, but in a good way."

It's only been two weeks since I've seen Marques.

I realize something important: my energy is at the same level as Marques. We 'see' each other now. We've always enjoyed each other's company, but now this shift in energy has connected us along the same energetic vibration.

I look at Marques and say, "I know how much you love yourself now."

It feels GOOD to love myself at last!

୪

When we walk in a blizzard, our eyes are blinded by swirling snowflakes so that we cannot see what is right in front of us. When that blizzard is going on in our minds, we cannot separate distracted thoughts from clear perception. The storm has to end first.

At the beginning of my dating frenzy, I dated a man who I summarily dismissed as not fitting the vision of what I was looking for in a man. My vision of the man I sought more closely aligned with Z; a man who would routinely ignore and abandon me, who would be 'too cool' to waste his time on me. I sought this type of man to punish myself, because I knew I was not worthy of love.

I know now that I am worthy of love. I don't need another person to love me to know I am worthy of love. I love myself deeply and fully.

Curiosity awakens about this man, K, who I summarily dismissed as not being mean enough. He was on my confessions call list, and he took the news well; in fact, he congratulated me for digging deep and pulling out honesty.

So one evening after church I invite K to dinner, as friends, to talk. What I learn about myself renews my commitment to myself to remain awake and authentic.

"What really broke my heart Kerri," K says, "Was when you told me over dinner one night that you were essentially traveling around the country having sex with other men while you were dating me."

I allow this truth to sink in. I allow the space for recognition of his pain that I caused with my callousness, during a time when all I could do was think about myself and my own desires.

"I am so deeply sorry for hurting you in this way," I tell him from the very core of my being. "I am surprised you would want to see me again."

"I saw you were going through a rough time," K says. "And I knew in my heart, that wasn't the real you."

We part ways after dinner with a hug and a kiss on the cheek.

"I'll wait for the end of your 100 days of celibacy," K says. "I'm here whenever you want to get together and talk, as friends."

෬

Feeling stronger and more determined inside, I throw out the first month of celibacy because I fell off three steps with David and I start over on my 100 days of celibacy. This time, I know I can commit to myself that I will complete the program faithfully. No more bargaining.

I am using the tools learned in Joshua Tree to keep myself strong on my path of transformation. And, I take a leap of faith in my journey: I cash out half of my SEP-IRA to pay off my car, to pay in advance for my education with the Four Winds, and to pay for my journey to Peru this summer. Everything feels in alignment, and I feel safe with Spirit.

On a lark, I start looking into when I can take the next course with the Four Winds since I have prepaid. Originally, I had decided I would not take the next course until November, but now I am feeling like I want the transformation to continue unfolding more quickly. I realize I can fly there for free with my airline miles, the class is already paid for, and I have the money necessary for room and board. Everything aligns perfectly, in true Spirit fashion, and I am on my way to Omega Institute in New York for a class in reading the signs of destiny.

One of the issues I have been grappling with in my mind and heart is that of intention versus letting it unfold. Lately I have read strategies of how to manifest what you want in your life (for example, Dr. Joe Dispenza), but I have also been hearing again and again this notion of relaxing and letting things unfold in your life according to Spirit. On the first day of class, as we are discussing destiny, I pose this question to Alberto Villoldo.

He answers with a roundabout story that concludes: "You set the intention and then let the Universe take care of the details. You don't need to trust that what you intend will happen. Maybe it will happen, maybe it won't. You just let go."

He continues. "See Kerri, you think you need to do everything or it won't happen. You don't trust. But you can't wait until you're <u>ready</u> to trust. You have to just let go and be open to see what happens next."

And there it is: the Easy button. Another layer of baggage is stripped away like a snake shedding its skin. I love it when he does that. I smile at him with eyes glistening, full of truth tears. "Thank you Alberto."

☙

As part of our learning at Omega, we work on individual sand paintings. I have come to love and respect the power of sand painting for the way it gives me insight into my life. Using tangible objects (a pine cone, some rocks or leaves, a stick, my finger in the dirt) to represent aspects or influences in my world, I can understand the forces that are affecting my experience of living. There's a magic that happens from this shift in perspective, from seeing my world laid out before me and from physically moving elements around so that they feel more balanced, or create greater harmony.

I am pulled to create my sand painting under a lovely bleeding heart plant. It feels as if those bright pink hearts speak to my own, as if they are promising to shower love and protection down on my sand painting, and into my life. As the week progresses, I notice that the longer the bleeding heart flower blooms, the more open it becomes. The blossom literally pulls apart at the seam, dropping its love down for all to see.

The bleeding heart blossom becomes a lesson for my own heart, to put down the armor and allow my heart to open and my love to be seen and felt by those around me. To lose my fear around opening. To trust.

I share my sand painting with two women from my class during a group exercise. It is like opening my diary and allowing them to read my soul. I open further and share my story with the class, my story of the bleeding heart and the lesson of opening and letting go. I speak up, as I often do, but really, I am not aware that anyone is actually listening.

Until the next morning. As I leave my dorm room for class, I notice a rolled up picture with a lovely silver bow outside my door. When I unfurl this gift, I discover a photograph of my bleeding heart flowers.

I gasp as my heart bursts open: *Someone 'heard' my soul talking.* I am overcome by the tenderness and care of a person who was so thoughtful as to leave me such a gift. I mean, to photograph my sand painting and go to the effort of printing it while on retreat?

On the way to class, I take a peek at my sand painting. A pine cone I had placed in my sand painting to represent the armor around my heart mysteriously disappeared overnight. Certainly it didn't blow away…

At class I am antsy, wanting to share this story and find out who gave me the picture. But there is not an opportunity at first. We are to get back into our groups from the day before and talk about our experience of viewing the sand paintings. When I join my group, Karen sees the photograph and confesses to leaving it. I am about to thank her when she says, "Yes, when I was leaving from home for this class, I felt like I had to bring this photograph. I just knew there was someone I was supposed to give it to. Then I realized it was for you Kerri."

Spirit heard my soul talking.

Spirit sent me to the bleeding heart because (as I find out later) this plant is healing for those who need to learn to love themselves and others unconditionally, with an open heart.

Spirit encouraged Karen to bring her photograph of the bleeding hearts and leave it for me so I would know I was heard, first by her and second by Spirit.

Spirit took away my pine cone, my armor.

The message was so clear:

Open your heart Kerri!

I see clearly how the synchronicity of these small events was masterfully orchestrated for the healing of one soul's heart. Now Karen's photograph serves as a reminder to me that I am held, and loved, and safe. I leave Omega at the end of the week knowing deep in my soul that I can open my heart wide and let my love shine out. Not only that, now I know for certain that it is my purpose.

&

When I return home from Omega I am totally charged up with energy and open. I have experienced new levels of perception that I did not even know I was capable of experiencing. I feel excited about all the possibilities in this new path with the Four Winds, and discovering more of my own innate abilities.

One thing I have noticed is that I am truly enjoying the company of the people in the Four Winds and my Thirteen Moons women's group and Spirit Paths. Essentially, I really enjoy spiritually conscious people.

I am taking a long hot bubble bath one night shortly after my return, relaxing and mulling over everything I learned at Omega, when I notice that the thoughts trickle out and my mind gets very still. Peace and quiet.

What happens next is simply amazing. With my eyes shut, relaxing, I see this periscope tunnel moving from far away and coming closer, closer and closer. Finally it gets right in front of my face and inside the circular end is the head of an Indian Chief or Medicine Man. He has a feathered headdress that reaches a foot above his face and down to his shoulders. He speaks:

Use your gifts to open the Sun.

And then the periscope pulls back, back, back until it finally disappears as I am calling out "Wait! Wait! What does that mean?"

I have a feeling my ancestry just made contact with me. I whip out my cellphone and look up Cherokee Chief headdress: I find a photo that shows a Chief wearing exactly the same sort of feathered headdress as the one I saw in my vision. The caption says it was worn by Chiefs and Medicine Men.

Whoa!

I breathe deeply and contemplate what that means. After a while, a spark of intuition occurs and I think it means that I need to use my writing and creativity and willingness to share with others to open the sunlight inside people's hearts and souls. To help people find the light who are in the darkness. Renewed purpose!

଄

The following Saturday at Thirteen Moons we explore our relationship with our parents. We learn about how we attach energetic cords to other people to create a false sense of security—especially to our parents. I have known about this concept through performing the Cutting the Cords ceremony with Kat, but it is interesting to know that I can cut my own cords to others with intention and ritual. When I feel into whether my body has energetic cords to my mother, I am surprised to find that there is one huge cord coming to my attention: it runs from my throat to my mother's root chakra. This cording makes perfect sense to me: My words affect my mother's sense of security in the world, so she has corded to my throat to try to make me stop speaking. As Chrispy later says, "Think about it: her root, your throat. What picture do you get? She's sitting on your neck."

In fact, I know I have often been afraid to speak my truth because I did not want to upset my mother or hurt her or worse…be judged by her.

I know this is a big cord, and they said not to tackle cords that are too big, but this one has got to GO! During the meditation, I visualize cutting the cord and holding both ends down to Pachamama for rooting. It feels at one point like it's too much for me to hold, like the cord is going to rebel and reattach itself. Suddenly I remember something Alberto Villoldo said about time not being linear, but happening all at once. That the past and future and the present are just concepts in our minds; that the present can affect the future, but also can affect the past. If this is true, then I am already a powerful Shaman, I decide, and therefore I can call on my 'future' more knowledgeable self to help me root these cords into the earth. When I call on Kerri, she comes on like a whoosh of powerful energy up my back and down through my arms, and I see the roots in those cords extending like golden threads into the earth. In a few minutes, the work is done, and I am surging from this rush of energy through my being.

With my eyes still closed, I am treated to a welcome vision: my mother and I are eating a picnic lunch under a big oak tree, laughing and talking. Oh I so wish that could happen someday. Maybe someday she can witness me for who I really am, and like what she sees.

In the meantime, it feels really good to have my throat unencumbered energetically. I feel like I can speak my truth now.

℞

There is a meditation and inquiry at Amala Foundation with Vanessa Stone one evening, and I choose to go to connect with the people who were on the retreat with me in February. I am curious if I have changed in their eyes, and if I will notice changes in myself by being around them again. I am about 80 days into my celibacy after starting over, and feeling very strong and grounded.

Hearing Vanessa speak again is delightful. She is filled with passion and love and wisdom, and offers insights for contemplation over the weeks to come. She has just published a book, and I venture to the café upstairs to have her sign a copy and talk for a few moments. When she sees me come into the room she smiles big.

"You are so different!" she showers me with praise. I accept it radiantly.

"Over 80 days of celibacy after starting over," I say. "I can't thank you enough for giving me that assignment. It changed the direction of my life. There's space for 'me' to emerge now."

"I see that," she says warmly. "You're glowing."

Although I know eventually I will not need validation from my teachers, right now it fills me with joy and pride. I climbed the pyramid and I found myself along the way. Only 20 days left to the top! I wonder what I will discover.

ͻ౪

One evening after Omega, the nightmare comes back. But this time, the volume of the white noise it creates is vastly diminished, and I am not afraid of it. I am inspired to say the Ho'oponopono prayer:

> *I'm sorry. Please forgive me. I love you. Thank you.*

I feel chills all over the left side of my ribcage, shoulder and arm. Then they pass, and I am peaceful enough to sleep.

ͻ౪

All of these things we do to ourselves that are painful, and then we tell ourselves to soldier on and deal with it and just move on…those places where we felt extreme sorrow or anger or betrayal or even joy and love—we lost energy in these places. If we pretend these situations and people and false beliefs never existed, if we do not accept them as places where we lost energy and reclaim ourselves, then these places haunt us and become our shadow.

To step into the light, we must review these events and reclaim our energy, reclaim our lost selves, reclaim our lost hopes and dreams, so that we can move forward in our lives with all of our Self present in this moment.

Every thought, word, and deed I have ever expressed in my life meant something—whether I realized it or not. Its meaning became deeper and more profound when I invested my emotions in it. I might think that what happened to me in high school cannot possibly be affecting me today; but it is. When I review the scenes in my mind during recapitulation[70], I see clearly all the places I lost energy trying to love Darren, trying to seek outside of myself for attention, engaging in loveless sexual acts. The patterns have repeated into my adulthood: those early experiences formed a shadow that created a predisposition, a longing, to repeat the same experiences.

Almost worse than losing my energy, is the realization that when I stuffed each of these experiences and simply moved on without acknowledging how deeply they hurt me, without reclaiming my energy and my Self, my heart became harder and harder, more and more closed to the feelings that are part of being a human engaged with life.

By adopting celibacy, I am able to pause the pattern so I can see it more clearly while preventing further damage to myself. Using recapitulation, I am able to witness the energy I lost and reclaim it to bring myself fully present and complete in the NOW. By witnessing where and how I lost energy to situations and people, I am able to remember my Self. By remembering my Self, I am able to regain trust that it is safe, that I can put aside the armor, and that I can open my heart.

I recapitulate every sexual encounter I have ever had with a man, especially those where I know I have given my heart and my sense of safety and stability to the man. Top on my list are Z, Robb, Andre, David, and of course, my cousin. I review every moment, every obsessive thought and desire, every place I notice I have lost energy being in relation to a man: I breathe back my Self, I breathe out what is not mine.

After I reclaim my energy, I sense where I have corded to the man and I cut those cords, sinking both ends deep into Pachamama, asking her to nourish the fears and needs that caused that cord to be created in the first place. I cord myself to Mother Earth for my sense of stability, and unconditional love and acceptance.

When I recapitulate the affair with my cousin, I witness all the ways I felt shame and abandonment and judgment. I witness the shame and judgment that do not belong to me, such as from my mother or my cousin, and I breathe that back to the Earth. I will not hold onto what is not mine to heal.

I recapitulate everything that feels juicy with regards to my cousin. Some of those memories involve my ex-husband, and I am careful to only recapitulate around him because I know in my heart that I am not ready to tackle a life review of my marriage to my best friend. All things in the right time will present themselves for healing. There is no rush. And so I focus on those things I can bear witness to without feeling all the saturated emotions that accompanied the memories in real life.

While I am not ready to recapitulate the twenty years with my ex-husband, I am ready to be a grown woman who is energetically separate from her mother. I cut every energetic cord that I feel running between my chakras and my mother's. There are cords almost at every chakra, even though I know I did a Cord Cutting with Kat not too long ago to separate from my mother. With purpose, and strong visualization and intent, I cut each cord and lovingly put the ends into Pachamama. I ask her to feed myself and my mother, to give each of us unconditional support, unconditional love, unconditional nourishment. Help us grow strong and independent, I ask the Mother. At some point in the future, I set intent that we will establish an un-corded relationship based on choice and love and mutual respect.

With all of the recapitulation and cord cutting I am performing, a ton of energy is being returned to my being. The energy needs to be directed to a purpose, an intention, because it is too vast an amount of energy for me to contain within my energetic body. Since my greatest desire is to help others who are now where I have been, to guide them from the darkness into the light, I visualize this memoir being published, I visualize speaking at workshops and signing books, I visualize seeing people's hearts open with glowing light, and I visualize lots and lots of hugs. I hold this clear intention, and I blow all of my returned energy into this new purpose. It feels poetic that the power of my memoir be fueled by the energy returned to me from the darkness of my shadow.

As I read, and re-read this memoir, I notice that I feel my experiences more deeply. At some points, I cry because...finally...my heart is opening again and I can feel now what I was not able to feel before. I feel immense compassion for myself and the struggle through my shadow. I feel great respect for myself and the courage it took to embark on this journey through the darkness, a hummingbird on an impossible journey. I feel powerful love for myself.

℆

There is another stop on the path of healing: forgiveness. I have been feeling pain in my lower right back, radiating into my hip and down my right leg all the way to the ankle. When I see my chiropractor, he takes an xray and tells me that a joint in my lumbar spine has arthritis and aging causing there to be tighter constriction around the nerves running through the joint—sciatica. The effects of this degeneration can be reversed with regular chiropractic work, but it takes time.

The yoga I have been doing feels like it has aggravated the condition, so I stop for a while and decide to see an acupuncturist since another friend solved a similar problem this way. At my first visit to an acupuncturist I close my eyes as she inserts the needles into various points in my body. I have no interest in witnessing needles being inserted into my flesh. It does not hurt, and when she is done she leaves the room to let my body clear its energy channels which the needles have left open. A half an hour later she removes the needles and I sit up. My entire body is flowing with energy in a way that I have never before experienced. Is this what I could feel like all the time?

I make another appointment, and I notice over the days that pass by that I feel far less pain than before in my back and hip. At the next appointment, I see a different acupuncturist; I am going to an acupuncture school for treatment because it is less expensive to be treated by student interns. This student acupuncturist inserts a long needle directly into the hip/buttock tissue where I feel the pain. After letting the needles do their work during this session, I notice I feel as if I do not have any issue in my hip or lower back when I arise from the table. It is amazing.

One thing is still gnawing at me though—why did this pain suddenly arise in my lower right back and hip around the time I started seeing Andre? And if the needles can move the energy and thereby erase this pain, then is it possible that this pain is actually caused by latent emotional energy that is stuck in my right hip? My friend who is a student at the acupuncture school tells me that one of the professors, Will, uses acupuncture for psychosocial healing as well as traditional healing. I book an appointment with Will, and after I've told him my theory he says this must be what is going on. I ask him how he knows and he says "Because you just told me so." He winks and smiles. "Our bodies know what is going on with them. As an acupuncturist, all I do is listen to the patient and then give them the healing pathway that their bodies already know they need."

He places the needles in my back as I lay face down on the table. When he leaves the room I open sacred space and call to Pachamama for healing. *Please help me release whatever needs to be released today so that my body can be relieved of this burden.* With my energy pathways open, I release all attachment to Andre, all hurt feelings having to do with our interactions, and I forgive myself and him for all trespasses. It feels like a weight has been lifted, and when Will returns he can feel the energy has shifted as well. He removes the needles and I flip over. More needles go into my top side.

Then he places a needle into the bottom of my foot, right into the pad between my big toe and second toe. It aches deep, deep down inside there and as the needle touches this place I gasp.

"You understand about repeating patterns, and how we get stuck on the original wound," Will says to me. "It's time to forgive it. Use this opportunity while your energetic channel is open to release it and forgive."

"It's time to forgive <u>that</u>??" I ask incredulously.

He nods and I start weeping as the realization hits me that this pain I feel in my foot is not physical pain, it is deep emotional pain. Not only do I feel it in my foot, but I feel it in exactly the area that hurts in my lower right back. I panic and start hyperventilating and crying and he is there to calm me down so that I can calm my fear and begin the work of breathing and the releasing.

It is time to forgive my father, to forgive Jack, for what he taught me to do in the tub. It is time to forgive my mother for the shame she had that I took on. It is time to forgive myself to taking responsibility, shame, and guilt for something that wasn't my fault.

"It wasn't my fault," I say.

"No. It wasn't," Will confirms.

I breathe in forgiveness, I breathe out shame, guilt, regret, and sadness. Waves of emotion surface as I breathe into this blocked energy, and I let it flow through me and out of my being.

Eventually, I am calmer and capable of managing the flow of this energy, and Will leaves the room to let me do the work.

At some point, Jack appears in my mind's eye. I look at him while I breathe out all that no longer serves, and breathe in forgiveness.

> *I forgive you Jack for what you did to me when*
> *I was just a baby. I don't know why you did this.*
> *But I forgive you.*
> *Now I need you to release me.*
> *Set me free Jack.*

I remember all the times I interacted with Jack throughout my life; they flash through my mind as I breathe. Then he looks deep into my eyes and smiles. He turns and walks away.

Now my mother appears in my mind's eye. There is so much weight here, and I breathe out the heaviness and breathe in forgiveness. Will steps in to check on me during this process, adjusts a few of the needles then adds a couple more. He winks at me.

"Those new needles will help with forgiveness."

Indeed, what felt blocked before feels like it can move now. I repeat to myself in a whisper:

> *I forgive you Mom.*
> *I love you.*
> *Please release me.*
> *Please set me free.*

I breathe out all energy belonging to her, releasing it. I breathe in forgiveness and love.

I feel energetically like my mother is resisting setting me free. I reach into my ancestry and I call on my grandfather; my grandfather used to come to my Mom in dreams and I know he is the only person she listens to.

Please grandpa. Please help Mom to let go of me. Visit her in her dreams. Help her to let go.

Now I realize I need to release all of my attachments to my mother. I need to set her free.

I am willing to release my need for my mother's love.
I am willing to release my need for my mother's approval.
I am willing to release my need for my mother's validation.
I am willing to release my need for my mother to understand me.
I am willing to release my need for my mother to agree with me.
I am willing to release my anger towards my mother.
I am willing to release my love for my mother.
I am willing to set my mother free.

I repeat a similar mantra for my Dad, because I realize I need to release my need for his love, his approval, his validation, and his understanding.

Afterwards, I feel tired from the work performed to release this deep wound. I also feel lighter from the many layers of my pain expunged. I am so very proud of myself for having the courage and fortitude to acknowledge and then release this deep wound. I realize I have shifted the destiny of my ancestral lineage. This ancestral wound stops with me—I have never abused my children, and now, I'm even helping to clean up the mess.

ℭ℘

100 days of celibacy accomplished. I climbed the 100 steps up the pyramid of celibacy without falling off once. The view at the top shows many possibilities for what to do with my sexual energy. But it was the journey that mattered most. Dedication to myself and belief

that I am worth it got me there, and by making it to the top I showed myself my strength.

∞

There is latent hostility and anger inside of me from all the years in my life that I suppressed it. I witness it when I play soccer, which is an aggressive sport, but I am pushing it even beyond those boundaries—cursing at other players on the field and getting really hot under the collar over minor things.

I've never liked expressing my anger. But when I tell Chrispy about these happenings, he tells me that is exactly what I must do. Cry, scream, pound pillows, hit a tree with a bat, throw rocks: whatever I need to do to move the energy out of me. I am so absolutely reluctant to do this.

"After everything else you've done, you don't want to do this?" Chrispy asks. "Maybe you need to read your own book again."

Later in the day, out of nowhere, comes the realization that I do not like expressing my anger because I don't want to be like my mother who expresses hers all the time. I didn't like being on the receiving end of it, and I don't want to do that to people I love. So I've associated having anger with not being my best self.

Hmmm. Picking apart this agreement I see that it is unrealistic to think that I will not ever feel anger. I am human, I will most definitely feel anger from time to time. And if I bottle it up and do not let it out, I will risk eventual physical ailment like the marriage cyst I had removed a year ago. So I need to express the emotions. But maybe there is a way in which I can let the anger out privately, without directing it at someone or affecting the people that I love with it.

In my darkened closet that night, I scream my rage into a paper cup. I scream and cry until my throat is hoarse and there are tears and snot all over my face. Then I cover that cup to seal it all inside. I intend to burn it on a sacred personal fire, let the fire transform and purify it, and then return all that energy...my energy...to myself for new purpose. This feels extremely empowering. Perhaps anger and I can have a productive relationship after all.

ॐ

Fluffy white cotton balls are stuffed all inside me as a protective layer. Or maybe the batting is more like clouds because I can blow it around as I lay on the table, my energetic channels opened with needles that Will has placed to allow the flow of whatever needs to leave, to go. I find myself breathing in, and then blowing these clouds out of my being, down through my feet where energy swirls warmly. The more I blow these clouds out, the more I realize there is something lurking underneath them, something I've been protecting.

And then I see her. She is lying on a bed in a meadow, resting like Sleeping Beauty. Her strawberry blonde curls pile up above her head and cascade over the edge of her resting place. She wears a silken azure gown like a princess or goddess, and all around her are lovingly placed flower blossoms in white, pink, red, gold, and lavender. She sleeps peacefully in glowing sunshine under all those clouds, protected by sacred trees that encircle and watch over her.

I realize I surrounded her in all this cotton, all these clouds, to protect her from the world I found myself living in: a world I decided was frightening; a world I decided was harsh and critical; a world I decided was empty and barren of meaning; a world I decided was threatening my deepest hopes, dreams, and desires.

I am careful to blow gently, to remove only as many clouds as is safe to disperse at this time, to gently wake her from her slumber, her frozen cocoon. I figure perhaps it will take many sessions on this table, with my energy channels opened, for me to blow away all these clouds so that she can awaken.

And then she opens her eyes and sees me. Her eyes sparkle green with wisdom beyond my own, and she smiles as she gazes at me lovingly.

I realize that it is I who is coming home to her.

ॐ

Each of us has a divine duty to strip away all that is not true to our being, and fully step into our personal authenticity. What is not authentic, what is not our true nature, is the very root cause of the suffering in ourselves and in this world. The distracted, spinning mind that spews untruths in a web of deceit through which we attempt to fathom the world around us—this mind needs to be quieted so that the soft whispered truths of Spirit, with messages of love, understanding, and peace can be heard.

Life is achingly simple: share love from your heart center with yourself and the world around you. When you come from heart center, even your work in the world can be an act of love. Returning to heart center is a spiraling journey of faith and disillusionment, of action and inertia, of release and renewal, of two steps forward and one step back.

You have witnessed my journey, so you know the path to transformation is not easy or straightforward. You just have to keep walking and trust that the transformation is occurring, just as when you see a flower bud emerge you trust it will unfold into a blossom.

The last evening at Joshua Tree retreat I was walking back to my dorm from the spiritual center, and I was feeling sad that the retreat was over and I would have to return to my normal life. I was feeling fearful about all it might mean to go back home. The labyrinth called to me in the starlight; its entrance beckoned. So I started walking the path. As I walked the path, I noticed the center and wondered which pathway around the labyrinth would lead me there. I would start predicting: the next turn I'll be at the center! And then the next turn would be further away from center instead. Finally! I made it to the center.

And you know what? Well…I started back from whence I came. See, that's how it works. The whole experience of life is walking the labyrinth, or climbing the pyramid—the work is to walk the path, or climb step by step. What changes is not the path. What changes is you. What changes is your perspective and your understanding about yourself and the world within which you live.

So take the first step. That is where the most amazing journey begins—the journey to YOU.

Suggestions

Try Energetic Shifting! Trying to shift your repeating patterns by talking about it is like trying to take a step forward when there is a concrete block cemented to your foot. There are many ways to energetically shift:

- make a sand painting or a mesa on the earth that represents your life and then tweak it over several days
- make a vision board for where you want your life to go using magazine cut-outs
- write troubles on paper or blow difficult emotions into paper, then burn it to release
- walk on fire and feel the awesomeness of fire filling your being with transformative energy
- do a tarot card or runes reading for yourself periodically to gain insights from Spirit and messages to carry forth in your daily life
- visit a Shaman or Reiki energy worker and get an energy shifting service

Find the Gifts In Your Woes! There are gifts that even the most difficult situation delivers to your doorstep, if you are only willing to open the door and receive. Assume that everything happens for a reason. Be _determined_ to discover that reason. Uncover the gifts, and you open a new chapter in your life where those gifts will come in handy.

Keep Pouring In Clear Water! Be willing to try anything to heal yourself, and keep doing it! My transformation eventually got to self-love because I never relented. I kept trying every retreat, spiritual methodology, energy healing, and workshop that I could find to keep pouring the healing into myself. Of course, this means many periods during which I felt bogged down as the detritus surfaced right before it was expelled. Visualize that you are a glass filled with sludge into which you are pouring clean water; that sludge will surface on its way out—on its way _OUT_. Bless and praise it as it goes away, and take the lessons to chart a better life course.

Balance with Essential Oils

One practice that helped me transform my mental, emotional, and physical body was the daily use of essential oils and supplements. When I went to the Be The Change conference in October 2012 (this is when I first walked on fire with HeatherAsh Amara), I began taking the doTerra Lifelong Vitality Complex which is a daily set of vitamins, minerals, botanical extracts, and omega fatty acids.

After four months of taking these daily supplements, I was strong and balanced enough in my health that I could stop taking Cymbalta which is an SSRI I was taking for depression and anxiety. I had been taking medication for depression since my first son was born...13 years of being medicated for having emotions.

Now I am chemical-free. I am happy, and emotionally stable, and mentally clear. I did the hard work to process my emotions, move my energy, make conscious decisions about my life, and get my body and mind healthy. **Question whether you <u>need</u> drugs to make yourself happy.**

Quotes

"Your Life, exactly as it is, is the perfect prescription for the evolution of your soul. This is an invitation to deepen into the Heart of Living, return to what is essential, redefine the purpose of this Life and realize the gift within this human experience." — Vanessa Stone

"The shaman is a self-realized person. She discovers the ways of Spirit through her inner awakening."
— Alberto Villoldo[71]

"Being hungry is about awakening and becoming conscious about our thoughts and feelings and actions. It's not about the hunger for food, but the craving to reclaim and embrace our true identity. About finding ways to be kind and compassionate to parts of ourselves that we dislike, dishonor, or which bring us shame."
— Dr. Robin Smith, Super Soul Sunday, Oprah

"There are two ways of spreading light. To be the candle, or the mirror that reflects it." — Edith Wharton

"Be responsible for your garden of life. The flowers from your garden will be cut, placed in a vase, and displayed in your home. You will smell them and see them everyday. Be aware of what's in your garden and be aware of the seeds you are planting." — don Jose Ruiz

"Give yourself the gift of being your own mother and saying yes to your own will, yes to your own wishes, yes to your own longings. Then, follow that path."
—Dr. Robin Smith, Super Soul Sunday, Oprah

"Your task is not to seek for love, but merely to seek and find all the barriers within yourself that you have built against it." — Jalal ad-din Rumi

"If you're still looking for that one person who can change your life, take a look in the mirror."
— Roman Price

Hummingbird Flight

It has been eight months since I sent this book to my reviewers, and the story contained within these pages is already a lifetime away.

Sitting this morning in my garden on a chilly February morning, I am meditating about birthing this memoir and completing my mission promised in so many prayers to Spirit. Re-reading my own story as I make edits to the manuscript brings tears to my eyes—I have immense compassion for the suffering endured, and if I had not written it down, I am not sure I would believe today all of the chain of events documented within these pages. Yet, it is so.

In the middle of these thoughts, I am interrupted by a humming sound and I open my eyes to discover the Spring's first hummingbird. She hovers nearby, drinking from the nectar I left for her many months ago before winter descended. Spirit whispers, *Fly little hummingbird! It's time for your next journey…*

Over the past eight months, a great deal more healing has occurred, catapulting me over the threshold from momentarily tasting self-love, into immersing in the experience of loving and accepting myself fully as an independent, single woman who has many, many potentials.

I am currently in the midst of writing my next book, *From Serial Monogamist to Independent Goddess*. After having read this book, I think you can surmise the contents of this new project. Of course, I am dating; however, the focus of my life is maintaining the integrity of my Self and the balance of my overall life.

Now when I date men, I have clear intentions of the space I am looking to fill in my life, and I have a strong boundary and container for myself. I am not changing myself to be in relationship with another person. I am solidly myself, and when I go on a date, I am evaluating how well the man fits who I am and the role I desire to fill. Because I have a relationship with my authentic self, I know who I am, and I do not lose myself when exploring relationships with others. A first date now is often like a one-on-one networking session;

it is simply an opportunity to get to know someone new and see if there is interest for a second date.

Of course, there has been occasion that feelings have deepened requiring great faith that I am safe even in my vulnerability. I experienced such a deep, rich, spiritual and passionate connection with a man, M, that it took all my faith to walk away from this connection when it became clear that the conditions under which the relationship had to unfold were distressful for me and would eventually become destructive of my happiness. I was able to walk away, maintaining the truth of the love at the same time as I held and nourished my own valid needs. I was able to stand strong, believing in myself, and trusting that, when the time is right, my heart's desire will be fulfilled, uncompromised.

The healing described in this book took time to unfold, along with additional experiences that fueled further transformation towards developing a solid, grounded Self.

Among these experiences was a trip to Peru during which I was blessed to spend nearly two weeks praying and diving deep into personal transformation with Marcela Lobos, Alberto Villoldo's partner, a group of amazing spiritual beings, and our Shaman, Don Martin. It was during this voyage that Pachamama reconnected me to her love and nurturing energy. The temple at Uno Uku, with its round stone and mud walls, beckoned me up the hill; and upon approaching the doorway to her sacred space, I felt an overwhelming rush of energy that can only be described as *Mother*. Into the womb of this temple I crawled on hands and knees, placed my forehead to the ground, and begged for forgiveness.

Please forgive me for forsaking my mother.
Please forgive me for taking for granted all the gifts you gave to me,
Pachamama.
Please forgive me for always wanting more.
Please forgive me for wanting to end my life.

Pachamama responded by reconnecting me energetically with a vibration that felt like a jackhammer under the Earth, pulsating nurturing life force up through the ground and into my feet, ankles, calves, and knees. Pachamama gave me legs to stand on my own.

In the days that followed, our Shaman, Don Martin, helped me move past a debilitating block to my progress—my own self-doubt. In a private healing session, he took from me what remained of my self-doubt, strengthening my Manipura, my third chakra, my seat of personal power. Working together—my intent and his spiritual connection—I was able to finally *believe* in myself.

As the West direction at the Four Winds Light Body School approached, I stepped up practice as a healer, offering to perform the Illumination service in exchange for testimonials. What I discovered was a very real ability to work as a shamanic practitioner, and a sense of profound purpose when helping others to transform their lives from suffering into fulfillment. As I stepped into the role of healer, I healed myself as well with acts of service.

These energetic, mental, and emotional shifts led me to an opening through which my mother and I were able to reconnect. Cautiously at first, we spoke carefully to one another over the phone, protecting the fragile nature of our new beginning. Success with telephone communication led to a first in-person meeting. Intentions very clear, we attempted a family gathering to celebrate my eldest son's birthday. Keeping the focus on my son, I brought his baby book and we adored photos and stories of his beginnings in this world. This successful reconnection led to my younger son's birthday, and a second reconnection of our family.

Another deep transformation occurred at the Four Winds class for the West direction. In the West direction, we explored inherited ancestral and karmic patterns that propel us toward a certain destiny. I was pulled to work with the ancestry of my natural father, and in the many spiritual exercises of the week I came to understand Jack and heal the wounds created in my early childhood. His energetic was given permission to speak to me in one exercise and the first words uttered were "I'm sorry Kerri". By working with his energetic, I came to understand that his soul grieved for the impacts that his wounded physical/emotional/mental bodies inflicted on my toddler self. I also came to awareness of the immense love that he held for me—a love that had no boundaries.

As the week progressed, I was given the opportunity to mourn his death with a ceremonial funeral. Since I did not attend his funeral when he died decades ago, this ceremony afforded me the spaciousness to grieve his loss, to honor his life, and to come to terms with the profound catalyst he was to my eventual transformation into the healer I am becoming—to my purpose on this Earth.

Most surprising of all, I discovered that Jack's spirit had been living inside of me since his death. I never really felt like he died. In fact, right after his passing I kept thinking I saw him on the streets of Northampton. I would see him behind me on the street, he would wink and grin, I would blink my eyes and refocus, and he would be gone. My feeling was so strong that he was still alive that I even tried researching it years later to see if his social security number was still in use.

When my classmates combined forces to practice on me the extraction process, I tested positive for a fluid entity which is a consciousness that can become lodged in your energy field when it passes from physical existence; in other words, when a person dies and they 'go to the light', sometimes that light is you. As they encouraged the energy to leave my being, I became distinctly aware that it was, in fact, Jack. He was waiting for something, hesitating. Then, I heard a little girl's voice, my voice, tell Jack "I love you Daddy"...*and whoosh!* The moment the words were uttered inside of me, my classmates extracted the entity. Grief descended as the extraction process finished; finally, he had left this world, and I felt the loss of him. Inside of me, it felt eerily quiet and spacious and vulnerable and uncomfortably *different*. Over the coming weeks, my soul grew to fill the space inside of me, and my balance and peace and joy returned.

With such a profound experience, came questions. Which parts of my thinking and behaviors were from him? Who was I now that he was gone? What was it like for him to be inside of me for over 20 years?

Who would I become now that it was only 'me' inside of me? Contemplation revealed a deep truth: it was his karma to witness the effects of his actions on my toddler self, from inside of me, helpless to do anything about it. If there is hell on Earth, I truly believe that would be it.

Following the extraction, my energetic had changed significantly once again, and that shift created the possibility for deeper healing with my parents. With Jack out of the energetic equation, relations with my parents were significantly eased. At my step-Dad's birthday, he gave me the most precious gift a father can give his daughter: forgiveness. He held my hands across the table at his birthday lunch, eyes glistening with love and forgiveness, and he energetically and verbally forgave me.

The Christmas holiday was spent gathered around the tree in my home, just like the year before. Except this time, there was even more for which to be thankful: I thought I had lost my family forever, and now I had them all gathered around me. I would have never suspected that cutting all ties to my parents would have led to an even deeper respect and connection with them; and yet, that is what happened, all because of my commitment to doing the daily energetic work to release and transform.

A very profound healing also occurred in my relationship with my ex-husband. I performed significant energy work to release the story of my marriage with gratitude, including a sacred fire at which I blew into a wedding photograph all the love, blessings, gratitude, and life experience I shared with this man, and then set it lovingly onto the fire. As I watched our smiling faces bubble and burn, I felt that part of my life being released to the flames. With unfettered gratitude in my heart, I was able to embrace his new life and love. On Christmas day, I gave him a card addressed to him and his new paramour, and inside I thanked her for being so loving towards my sons. I shared my gratitude that Tom had selected such a kind and generous woman as his partner. I also thanked Tom for everything he does to help our sons grow up healthy, strong, and wise. I unclenched my heart and allowed him to be free to love again. I also set myself free.

The healing continues to unfold in my primary relationships, especially with my mother. How can we reconcile that we each remember the event of our discord so differently—words spoken and actions taken—that it seems we do not remember the same event? The answer: We cannot 'figure out' who was right or wrong; the question is irrelevant and impossible to determine. We remember the event differently because we each are operating from our own world view, our own perceptual filters.

"We don't see things as they are,
we see things as we are". –Anais Nin

So rather than futilely trying to make match these differing accounts of our disagreement, we must proceed with heightened awareness and respect for one another, we must avoid pushing the buttons even though we certainly know how to, and we must employ exit strategies that prevent tensions from raising that high again.

ന

At the North direction with the Four Winds, the mystery of my nightmares was revealed to me. A fellow student journeyed into my subconscious mind and found a vision of me as a child playing in a room filled with shadows, a single spotlight of pure white light cast down upon me where I played. Another light came from a window and she saw my little girl walk over and take a look outside at all the other children playing outside. Then I walked back to my spotlight in the middle of shadows to play by myself. She also found a contract that had been written for me, a soul contract. It was written on a scroll with pen and ink, and in big letters it said: I AM. Fading in and out underneath this bold statement was: NOT. When I explored this vision and contract in a group activity designed by the Four Winds, I discovered a voice within me that had the same energetic signature as the terror that gripped me during my nightmares, and I realized this voice, this presence, was keeping me trapped in a state of being that could never move forward, never succeed.

In front of the class of nearly 60 people, my teacher extracted this contract from my subconscious mind, a curse placed upon me and still enforced by dark energetic presences that had no right to do so. As I was liberated from this curse, my body shook and my teeth rattled uncontrollably and I cast off the energetic spell that had bound me to suffering my entire life. It sounds so unreal to any person who has never experienced such a thing, and yet it has freed me to finally believe that I AM. I can be anything I choose to be. And I no longer have to hide in the shadows playing by myself. Before this experience, my essential self was submerged under water inside of me. Having a conversation was exhausting because my true self had to struggle up through what felt like an ocean just to be heard. Now my essential self can live at the surface, can engage directly with life all around me, and it is effortless in comparison. I am finally able to be present in every moment, hearing what my children are saying to me and really noticing the nuances of their expressions. I remember what people say to me and experiences we share, whereas before I was hiding so deep within myself that the outside world was irrelevant. In fact, it is now awkward for me when I see people who have known me for years and they remember my name, but I have no idea what their name is. I remind myself that I did the best I could at the time, and that I am blessed that now I have the ability to witness people and situations outside of myself, and because there is less struggle going on inside of me, I can be vastly more engaged with the world around me.

At the North direction I was also given the opportunity to transform my relationship to the diagnosis of borderline personality disorder. As I worked with the word borderline using my body and emotions, and I brought it through all facets of my perception and awareness, I transformed it into border-*less*, and then finally to *boundless*.

☙

To come full circle with all the experiences I describe in this memoir, Spirit sent me a special gift so I could witness for myself the deep healing that had taken place inside of me. In rare cases, you meet a life-size mirror of yourself so that you can fully experience yourself as others do. I had the honor of meeting such a mirror, and while the experience was intense, it was also extremely validating and insightful. Through interaction with my mirror, I was able to fully experience my former wounded self—the self who made assumptions, who took things personally, who could not respect boundaries, and who did not love myself (even though I thought I did at the time!). My mirror enabled me to feel the effects of my former self from my newer, more healed self; I could feel my former self's powerful desire to be loved and accepted along with my former loneliness, rejection, hopelessness, and general yuckiness when the object of my desire did not reciprocate. Overwhelming feelings of compassion for my former self and my mirror mixed with gratitude for the journey that has led me to a more healed state where love and acceptance do not need to come from outside of myself. I have now stood on both sides of this mirror: I have compassion for my former self and how I struggled inside myself to feel worthy of love, and at the same time I finally understand how and why my longing and desperate need for love pushed away the very person whose attention I craved. I finally know how it felt to be the target of my powerful needs. Because of this experience, I know without a doubt that I have significantly healed along my journey, and I know the kind of lover I wish to be in the future. While it is always a difficult situation when two people part ways, it is with gratitude that I wave goodbye to my mirror; he has been my most significant teacher, allowing me to come full circle to truly understand the journey I have undertaken.

∞

After so much profound healing, I felt I should have been ready to take on the world. But there was still a deep fear that all of this healing was an illusion and at any moment the suffering would return. I also had significant concern that my children would be consumed by the same shadows that had overtaken me for so much of my life. At the next class with the Four Winds, I worked through these fears and grappled with my shadow. I did a sand painting to energetically push back the shadow into my past so that its reach does not extend into the future with my children. The curse that haunted me my entire life had no business going after my kids, and mama bear wasn't going to let it.

Because Spirit is generous and loving, a message was conveyed to me through an exercise with a fellow student at the Four Winds. My question of Spirit (not shared with the student) was "Did I get that shadow out by the roots?" The answer was a vision of a powerful mountain behind me, strengthening me; this, I knew, was the lineage of which I had become a part with the Four Winds. And the student then said, "There are new roots growing in front of this mountain."

∝

As I reflect upon this memoir and the story of my life, I am grateful for taking the first step in a journey of a thousand miles. I am grateful for persevering even when I reached rock bottom.

I am grateful to myself for seeking and accepting help. I am grateful for the constant guidance and nurturing from family, friends, mentors, and especially...Spirit.

Thank you dear Hummingbird, for making the
impossible journey, outside of time, to change your Destiny.

A Final Wish

If any part of my story has touched your heart, or resonated with your personal experience, I encourage you to unburden yourself of shame and embrace love. I encourage you to try any number of the suggestions in this book to start or continue your own journey of healing. I encourage you to believe, beyond hope, that when you reach out from the shadows a hand will grasp yours and pull you into the light.

We are all walking the same path. Some of us are a few steps ahead, some a few steps behind. Those ahead of us have the privilege of calling out "pothole ahead!" to keep us from tripping up on the same obstacle.

It may seem impossible to even attempt to go on a journey of spiritual awakening. But as Laozi says, "A journey of a thousand miles begins with a single step." Take the first step. Spirit will send help just when you need it.
It will be hard at times to keep taking steps. Keep hope in your heart.

Keep walking the path. A brighter day will come if you believe.

Resources

[1] *The Gifts of Imperfection*, Brené Brown

[2] "There is a crack in everything. That's how the light gets in." Leonard Cohen

[3] *Only*, Nine Inch Nails

[4] *Stellar*, Incubus

[5] *Heartless*, Kanye West

[6] *The Gifts of Imperfection*, Brenè Brown

[7] *The Power of Now*, Eckhart Tolle

[8] Laozi, also known as Lau-tzu, was reputedly the author of the *Tao Te Ching*, a significant work of Chinese cosmogony, and was a philosopher of ancient China from 6th century BCE.

[9] *Spirit Paths: The Quest for Authenticity*, Gerry Starnes, M.Ed

[10] *Radical Acceptance*, Tara Brach, Ph.D.

[11] *The Toltec Path of Transformation*, HeatherAsh Amara

[12] *The Healing Power of the Breath*, Richard Brown and Patricia Gerbarg

[13] Allan Hardman, Relationship Coach, *Interview with TOCI* November 2012

[14] *RockStarYoga* blog, Chrispy Bhagat Singh, www.rockstaryoga.us

[15] *The Gifts of Imperfection*, Brenè Brown

[16] *The Gifts of Imperfection*, Brenè Brown

[17] *The Gifts of Imperfection*, Brenè Brown

[18] *Spirit Paths: The Quest for Authenticity*, Gerry Starnes, M.Ed

[19] *A Quiver of the Heart*, Sharon Salzberg

[20] *The Toltec Path of Transformation*, HeatherAsh Amara

[21] *RockStarYoga* blog, Chrispy Bhagat Singh, www.rockstaryoga.us

[22] *The Six Sacred Gifts*, Cecilia Zuniga

[23] *The Four Agreements*, Don Miguel Ruiz

[24] *The Mastery of Love*, Don Miguel Ruiz

[25] "Indiana Jones and the Last Crusade," Harrison Ford as Indiana Jones

[26] Reiki is a Japanese technique by which a practitioner moves unseen life force energy through a person.

[27] *The Six Sacred Gifts*, Cecilia Zuniga

[28] *Daring Greatly: How the Courage to Be Vulnerable Transforms the Way We Live, Love, Parent, and Lead*, Brené Brown

[29] *Courageous Dreaming: How Shamans Dream The World Into Being*, Alberto Villoldo, PhD

[30] *RockStarYoga* blog, Chrispy Bhagat Singh, www.rockstaryoga.us

[31] 20 Feet Tall, The New Amerykah Part Two, Return of the Ankh, Erykah Badu

[32] *The Seven Habits of Highly Successful People,* Stephen Covey

[33] *The Toltec Path of Transformation,* HeatherAsh Amara

[34] *The Toltec Path of Transformation,* HeatherAsh Amara

[35] *The Mastery of Love,* Don Miguel Ruiz

[36] *The Gifts of Imperfection,* Brenè Brown

[37] *The Six Sacred Gifts,* Cecilia Zuniga

[38] *RockStarYoga* blog, Chrispy Bhagat Singh, www.rockstaryoga.us

[39] *The Book of Runes,* Ralph H. Blum

[40] *The Book of Runes,* Ralph H. Blum

[41] *Spirit Paths: The Quest for Authenticity,* Gerry Starnes, M.Ed

[42] *Spirit Paths: The Quest for Authenticity,* Gerry Starnes, M.Ed

[43] *Animal Spirit Guides,* Steven D. Farmer, PhD.

[44] *The Gifts of Imperfection,* Brenè Brown

[45] *The Lotus and the Lily,* Janet Conner

[46] *The Six Sacred Gifts,* Cecilia Zuniga

[47] Personal email from Chrispy Bhagat Singh

[48] *The Six Sacred Gifts,* Cecilia Zuniga

[49] *Mending the Past and Healing the Future with Soul Retrieval,* Alberto Villaldo, Ph.D.

[50] *Spirit Paths: The Quest for Authenticity,* Gerry Starnes, M.Ed

[51] Quote from the *Matrix* motion picture (1999)

[52] "Pelican," Animal Speak, The Spiritual & Magical Powers of Creatures Great & Small, Ted Andrews

[53] "Lobster," Animal Speak, The Spiritual & Magical Powers of Creatures Great & Small, Ted Andrews

[54] "Fox," Animal Speak, The Spiritual & Magical Powers of Creatures Great & Small, Ted Andrews

[55] "Wolf," Animal Speak, The Spiritual & Magical Powers of Creatures Great & Small, Ted Andrews

[56] "Bear," Animal Speak, The Spiritual & Magical Powers of Creatures Great & Small, Ted Andrews

[57] "Raven," Animal Speak, The Spiritual & Magical Powers of Creatures Great & Small, Ted Andrews

[58] Thanks to my friend Mike for this comment! Ha!

[59] *The Keys to the Kingdom,* David Owens Ritz

[60] *Spirit Paths: The Quest for Authenticity,* Gerry Starnes, M.Ed

[61] *Breaking the Habit of Being Yourself,* Dr. Joe Dispenza

[62] "Raven," Animal Speak, The Spiritual & Magical Powers of Creatures Great & Small, Ted Andrews

[63] *Breaking the Habit of Being Yourself*, Dr. Joe Dispenza

[64] *The Keys to the Kingdom*, David Owen Ritz

[65] *The Four Agreements*, Don Miguel Ruiz

[66] *Breaking the Habit of Being Yourself*, Dr. Joe Dispenza

[67] *Sticking With It*, Sharon Salzberg

[68] *Hang On to Your Ego*, Thanissaro Bhikkhu, Tricycle Magazine, Summer 2007

[69] "Vulture," Animal Speak, The Spiritual & Magical Powers of Creatures Great & Small, Ted Andrews

[70] Recapitulation is a Toltec practice I learned from HeatherAsh Amara as part of the 13 Moons program. It is a powerful way of reclaiming energy lost to situations or people using the power of your intent and breath.

[71] *Shaman, Healer, Sage: How to Heal Yourself and Others with the Energy Medicine of the Americas*, Alberto Villoldo

CPSIA information can be obtained at www.ICGtesting.com
Printed in the USA
LVOW01s1951191014

409490LV00029B/1094/P

9 780615 897981